THE SIMPLE CONVECTION OVEN COOKBOOK

+90 EASY & HEALTHY RECIPES FOR ANY CONVECTION OVEN. | GET THE MOST OUT AND ENJOY YOUR MEALS.

ALICIA MURPHY

CONTENTS

Introduction ix

BREAKFAST

1. Baked Croissant Breakfast Sandwiches — 3
2. Tasty Crab Quiche — 5
3. Muffin and Egg Casserole — 7
4. Basil Cheese Frittata — 9
5. Egg and Bacon Muffin Cups — 11
6. Easy Oven Omelets — 13
7. Ham, Cheese and Bacon Quiche — 14
8. Caramel Apple Buttermilk Muffins — 16
9. Roasted Butternut Squash and Red Onion — 18
10. Soft Dinner Rolls — 20
11. Breakfast Pita Bread — 22
12. Yukon Potato, Leek and Feta Frittata — 24

LUNCH

13. Mozzarella Pita Melts — 29
14. Roasted Grape and Goat Cheese Crostini — 31
15. Parmesan-Crusted Pork Chops — 33
16. Pecan-Crusted Catfish — 35
17. Roasted Mini Peppers — 37
18. Moroccan Pork Kebabs — 39
19. Herb Baked Chicken Tenders — 41
20. Healthy Oven Roasted Potatoes — 43
21. Honey Balsamic Chicken Breasts And Veggies — 44
22. Baked Garlic Fries — 46
23. Tomato Avocado Melt — 48
24. Roasted-Fennel Ditalini and Shrimp — 50

PORK, BEEF AND LAMB

25. Baked Ham and Cheese Rollups	55
26. Pork Rolls with Teriyaki Sauce	57
27. Keto Pork Chops Parmesan Breading	59
28. Pulled Pork Carnitas Quesadillas	61
29. Crispy Pork Wontons	63
30. Tuscan Pork Chops	65
31. Parmesan Baked Pork Chops	67
32. Pork Satay with Peanut Dipping Sauce	68
33. Vietnamese Caramel Pork	70
34. Beef Taco Egg rolls	72
35. Tasty Beef Stroganoff Casserole	74
36. Texas Oven-Roasted Beef Brisket	76
37. Baked Steak WithParmesan And Pepper Crust	78
38. Simple Steak	79
39. Corned Beef Egg Rolls	80
40. Thin-Sliced Breaded Top Round Cutlets	82
41. Tasty Garlic and Orange Juice Steak	84
42. Lamb Shanks with Olives And Capers	86

CHICKEN AND TURKEY

43. Jerk-Spiced Turkey Loaf	91
44. Ricotta and Parsley Rolled Turkey Breasts	93
45. Sweet and Sour Chicken	95
46. Honey and Wine Chicken Breast	97
47. Tasty Peru Chicken BBQ	99
48. Tasty Asian Chicken Wings	100
49. Tasty Almond Battered Chicken	102
50. Garlic Breaded Chicken Bake	104
51. Crusted Chicken Tenders	106
52. Buffalo Chicken Wings	107
53. Greece Chicken BBQ Skewers	108
54. Tasty Jerk Chicken Wings	110
55. Turkey Rice with Broccoli	112
56. Chicken Crunchies With Lemon Mayo	114

SEAFOOD

57. Oven-Roasted Sea Bass with Ginger and Lime Sauce	119
58. Baked Sardines With Garlic and Oregano	121
59. Shrimp Scampi Bake	123
60. Lemon Pepper Salmon	124
61. Roast Moroccan Fish and Vegetables with Spicy Couscous	126
62. Baked Sole with Mint and Ginger	128
63. Baked Swordfish Steaks	130
64. Crab Stuffed Haddock	132
65. Dijon Baked Salmon	134
66. Broiled Tilapia Parmesan	136
67. Baked Scallops	138
68. Baked Mexican Fish	140
69. Baked Tilapia With Buttery Crumb Topping	142

VEGETABLES

70. Tasty Jalapeno Poppers	145
71. Nutty Cauliflower Bites	147
72. Roast Cauliflower and Broccoli Florets with Garlic Dipping Sauce	149
73. Tasty Jicama Fries	151
74. Asparagus Strata	153
75. Baked Brussels Sprouts	155
76. Almond Flour Onion Rings	156
77. Avocado Fries	158
78. Roasted Vegetable Salad	159
79. Roasted Brussels Sprouts	161
80. Roasted Broccoli	162
81. Pineapple Coconut Brown Rice Salad	164

DESSERT AND APPETIZERS

82. Roasted BBQ Chickpeas	169
83. Flaky Buttermilk Biscuits	171
84. Brown Sugar Shortbread Caramel Bars	173

85. Sweet Spiced Pecans	175
86. Very Berry Pie	177
87. Cheddar Cheese Puffs	179
88. Feta and Zucchini Fritters with Garlic Yogurt Sauce	181
89. Black & White Brownies	183
90. Blueberry Muffins Recipe with Lemon Glaze	185
91. Apple Hand Pies	187
92. Easy Baked Glazed Chocolate Donuts	189
93. Raspberry Cream Cheese Sweet Rolls	191
94. Ginger Spice Cookies	193
95. Vegan Coconut Cake	195
96. Crème brûlée	197
97. Upside-Down Peach Cake	199

Copyright ©2021 by Alicia Murphy.

All Rights Reserved. Without limiting the rights under copyright reserved above; no part of this publication may be reproduced, stored in or introduced into a retrieval system, or transmitted, in any form, or by any means (electronic, mechanical, photocopying, recording, or otherwise), without the prior written permission of the copyright owner of this book.

INTRODUCTION

Convection ovens have been around since the 1950s and are commonly preferred over the conventional oven. The setback of the conventional oven is that it has stationary heating elements with no fans to circulate the heat generated. The hot air rises and settles on the surface, so the upper half of the oven would always be hotter than the lower half. If you plan to bake two sheets of cookies in the conventional oven, the cookies placed on the top rack would cook faster than the bottom half; almost a full 30 degrees hotter than the lower.

A convection oven has heating elements placed at both the top and bottom of the oven and also uses a fan to circulate the air within the oven to equalize the temperature, so no matter where you place the dish or how many dishes you cook at the same time, hot air is circulated continuously. This eliminates cold spots, cooks food evenly, renders fat more quickly, and caramelizes sugar faster among other benefits.

BREAKFAST

1

BAKED CROISSANT BREAKFAST SANDWICHES

Prep Time 15 minutes
Cook Time 15 minutes
Calories per Serving: 440
Serves: 8 yields

Ingredients

6 large eggs
8 slices deli ham
1/3 cup whole milk
Salt and pepper, to taste
8 croissants, sliced in half
8 sharp cheddar cheese slices
1/2 cup mozzarella cheese, shredded

Instructions:

1. Preheat oven to 325F.
2. Place the bottom half of the croissants on a large sheet pan. Place a ham slice and a slice of cheese on each of the croissant.
3. Combine the egg, milk the pepper and salt in a bowl and then pour into a greased skillet and cook for 3 minutes over medium heat, stirring with a wooden spoon and scraping the bottom of the pan as the eggs cook.

4 Add the mozzarella cheese and stir to melt and combine. Once eggs are cooked, remove from heat.

5. Scoop the scrambled eggs on the ham and cheese and top with the second half of the croissant buns.

6. Transfer to the preheated oven, place in the middle rack and bake for 5-10 minutes to melt cheese and toast croissants.

7. Remove from heat and set aside to cool for a few minutes before serving.

2

TASTY CRAB QUICHE

Prep Time: 5 minutes
Cook Time: 25 minutes
Calories per Serving: 150
Serves: 4

Ingredients:

1 pie crust
4 eggs, beaten
A pinch of salt
1 cup of heavy cream
1 teaspoon of hot sauce
2 cans of lump crabmeat
1 cup of shredded cheese
1/4 cup of grated parmesan cheese
1 medium yellow onion, chopped finely
1/4 teaspoon of freshly ground black pepper

Instructions:

1. Preheat the oven to 350F, arrange racks.

2. Place the pie crust on a 1 inch rack, and transfer to the preheated oven to bake on high until brown for about 5 minutes. Remove from heat and set aside.

3. Next, add the rest of the ingredients to a mixing bowl and stir until well combined.

4. Transfer the mixture to the pie crust, place in the oven to bake for 10 minutes.

5. Reduce heat to 300F and bake for an additional 10-15 minutes. Check doneness by inserting a toothpick to the center until it comes out clean.

3

MUFFIN AND EGG CASSEROLE

Prep Time: 10 minutes
Cook Time: 30 minutes
Total Time: 40 minutes
Calories per Serving: 320
Serves: 3

Ingredients:
1 package, 12 oz of English muffins
3 slices of bacon, roughly chopped
3 eggs, beaten
3/4 cup of skimmed milk
1 teaspoon of lemon zest
2 teaspoon of lemon juice
1 tablespoon of mayonnaise
Butter

Instructions:
1. Preheat the oven to 350F. Lightly coat a 4 x 4 inch baking dish with butter then split the muffins and chop them into 1 inch pieces, set aside.
2. Next, combine the eggs and milk in a large mixing bowl and whisk until fluffy.

3. Add the rest of the ingredients to the bowl and stir until well combined.

4. Gently dip split muffins into the bowl, mix until well coated.

5. Afterwards, pour the mixture into the baking dish and transfer to the middle rack of the oven to bake for 25-30 minutes until golden brown and a toothpick inserted in the center comes out clean.

6. Remove from heat and stand for 10 minutes before serving.

4

BASIL CHEESE FRITTATA

Prep Time: 10 minutes
Cook Time: 25 minutes
Total Time: 35 minutes
Calories per Serving: 146
Serves: 4

Ingredients:
1 tablespoon of olive oil
Salt to taste
8 eggs, beaten
1/2 cup of milk
1/2 cup of goat cheese
1/2 cup of fresh, chopped
6 oz of chopped sun dried tomatoes
1 medium yellow onion, chopped finely
1/4 teaspoon of freshly ground black pepper

Instructions:
1. Heat the olive oil in a saucepan set over medium heat, add onions and sauté until soft and translucent.
2. Next, combine the egg, milk, tomatoes, basil, onions and

goat cheese in a mixing bowl, stir to combine. Season with salt and pepper.

3. Transfer the mixture to a baking dish and place in the oven to bake for 20-25 minutes over heat set to 350F. Until a toothpick inserted in the center comes out clean.

4. Remove from heat and stand for a few minutes before serving.

5

EGG AND BACON MUFFIN CUPS

Prep Time: 10 minutes
Cook Time: 15 minutes
Total Time: 25 minutes
Calories per Serving: 113
Serves: 3

Ingredients:

6 eggs, beaten
1/2 cup of bacon crumbles
1/2 red bell pepper, seeds removed and chopped
4 tablespoons of milk
Salt and freshly ground black pepper, to taste
1/4 cup of cheddar cheese, shredded
*Requires a 6 cup muffin tray.

Instructions:

1. Lightly coat the muffin tray with cooking spray and set aside.

2. Combine eggs and the rest of the ingredients in a large mixing bowl and stir

3. Transfer mixture to the muffin cups and place tray on the 1 inch rack.

4. Cook with heat set to 350F for 12-15 minutes until a toothpick inserted in the center comes out clean.

5. Remove from heat and serve immediately.

6
EASY OVEN OMELETS

Prep Time: 10 minutes
Cook Time: 10 minutes
Total Time: 20 minutes
Serves: 2

Ingredients:

6 eggs, beaten
3 oz. of shredded cheddar cheese
1/2 cup of bacon
1/8 cup of onions, chopped finely
1 medium green pepper, seeds removed and chopped
1/2 tablespoon of fresh parsley, chopped

Instructions:

1. Add eggs and milk to a large mixing bowl and stir until well combined and fluffy.

2. Next add the cheese and the rest of the ingredients, stir to combine.

3. Transfer the mixture to your 4 x 4 inch baking dish and place in the oven. Set heat to 350F and bake for 10 minutes.

4. Remove from the oven and serve with English muffins. Enjoy your breakfast!

7

HAM, CHEESE AND BACON QUICHE

Prep Time: 10 minutes

Cook Time: 20 minutes

Total Time: 30 minutes

Calories per Serving: 220

Serves: 4

Ingredients:

Pie crust

3 eggs, beaten

1 cup of diced ham

1 tablespoon of flour

1 1/2 cup of skimmed milk

1 1/2 cup of shredded cheddar cheese

Salt and freshly ground black pepper to taste

Instructions:

1. Place the pie crust on the 1 inch rack, transfer to the oven and heat on high until brown for about 5 minutes. Remove from heat and set aside.

2. Top pie crust with a layer of ham, bacon and a fine drizzle of cheddar cheese, set aside.

3. Next, combine the rest of the ingredients in a mixing bowl and stir to mix well, pour the mixture over the pie crust.

4. Transfer pie crust to the lower rack of the oven, bake with temperature set to 350 F for 10 minutes, afterwards reduce heat to 300F and bake for 10 additional minutes. Check doneness by until a inserting a toothpick in the center to see if it comes out clean.

8

CARAMEL APPLE BUTTERMILK MUFFINS

Prep Time: 15 minutes
Cook Time: 20 minutes
Total Time: 35 minutes
Calories per Serving: 326
Serves: 16 (muffins)

Ingredients

For the streusel topping:
1 tablespoon of butter
1/3 cup firmly packed brown sugar
½ teaspoon ground cinnamon
½ cup finely chopped walnuts
For the muffins:
½ cup vegetable oil
1 1/3 cup packed brown sugar
1 egg
2 teaspoons vanilla extract
1 cup buttermilk
2½ cups all-purpose flour you may need a bit more, if the batter is too wet
¼ teaspoon salt

2½ teaspoons baking powder
½ teaspoon baking soda
1¾ cups coarsely chopped peeled apple

For The Caramel Icing:
2 tablespoon butter
¼ cup brown sugar
2 tablespoons milk
1 teaspoon vanilla extract
1 cup powdered sugar

Instructions:

1. Preheat the oven to 325F, line 16 muffin cups with muffin liners and set aside.

2. Combine all streusel topping ingredients in a mixing bowl and stir until you have a crumbly mixture, use your hands if necessary.

3. Next, combine the flour, baking powder, salt and baking soda in a separate mixing bowl, set aside.

4. Combine the oil, egg, sugar, milk and vanilla extract in another bowl, stir to mix well. Combine the vanilla mixture with the flour mixture and mix well. Add the chopped apples and mix well.

5. Spoon the batter into the prepared muffin cups and top with the streusel topping.

6. Place in the oven and bake for 15-20 minutes. Check doneness by inserting a toothpick in the center of the muffin to see if it comes out clean, if it doesn't, bake for an additional 5 minutes.

7. While the muffins bake, prepare the caramel icing; add the butter, brown sugar and milk to a microwavable bowl and stir until well mixed. Place in the microwave on high for 30 seconds.

8. Add vanilla and sugar and stir until smooth and slightly thick but not runny. Drizzle over muffins and serve, enjoy.

9

ROASTED BUTTERNUT SQUASH AND RED ONION

Prep Time: 10 minutes
Cook Time: 20 minutes
Total Time: 30 minutes
Calories per Serving: 325
Serves: 4

Ingredients:

1 tablespoon of ground cumin
1/2 teaspoon of cayenne pepper
1/4 teaspoon of ground nutmeg
1/2 teaspoon of ground coriander
1 tablespoon of light brown sugar
Kosher salt
2 small red onions
10 sprig of fresh thyme
2 small Butternut Squash
2 tablespoons of olive oil

Instructions:

1. Heat oven to 400F and lightly coat 2 large rimmed baking sheets with cooking spray and set aside.

2. Add the first 6 ingredients in a bowl and stir until well mixed.

3. Combine the rest of the ingredients in a bowl and divide among prepared baking sheet, divide the spice mixture and arrange neatly in a single layer.

4. Transfer baking sheet to the oven and roast until golden brown for 20-25 minutes.

10

SOFT DINNER ROLLS

Prep Time: 4 hours
Cook Time: 20 minutes
Total Time: 4 hours 20 minutes
Serves: 14 rolls

Ingredients:

1 teaspoon salt
1 large egg, beaten
1/4 cup unsalted butter
2 1/4 teaspoons of yeast
1 cup of warmed whole milk
2 tablespoons of granulated sugar, divided
3 cups of all-purpose flour

For the topping:

2 Tablespoons of melted unsalted butter
1 Tablespoon honey

Instructions:

1. Add the milk, yeast and sugar into a mixing bowl and whisk until it reaches dough like consistency. Sit covered for 10 minutes.

2. Stir in the egg, butter, 1 cup of flour, salt and the remaining sugar to the mixture and whisk until well incorporated. Add the

remaining flour and whisk until the dough comes together and thickens.

3. Remove dough from the bowl and knead on a smooth, clean and lightly floured surface.

4. Next, evenly oil a large bowl with olive oil, place kneaded dough in the bowl and cover for about 1-2 hours. This is to enable the dough rise and double in size.

5. While the dough rises, grease two 9 inch square baking pans with oil/cooking spray and set aside.

6. After about 2 hours, uncover the dough and pinch to release the trapped air. Divide into 14 equal pieces and shape each piece into a smooth ball like shape with your hands.

7. Transfer rolls to the prepared baking pan and cover for about an hour to enable it rise.

8. Space out the oven racks and preheat the oven to 325F.

9. Loosely tent the baking pan with foil then place in the oven to bake for 15-20 minutes until golden brown on top.

10 While the rolls bake, prepare the honey topping by combining both ingredients in a bowl. When the rolls are done, remove them from the oven and brush with topping. Set aside to cool for a few minutes before serving.

11

BREAKFAST PITA BREAD

Prep Time: 3 hours
Cook Time: 10 minutes
Total Time: 3 hours, 10 minutes
Calories per Serving:
Serves: 8 pita bread

Ingredients:
1 cup of warm water
1 ¾ teaspoons salt
1 cup of all-purpose flour
1 ¾ cups of all-purpose flour
1 teaspoon of olive oil, divided
.25 oz. of package active dry yeast
1 ½ tablespoons of extra virgin olive oil

Instructions:
1. Combine yeast, water and flour in a bowl and whisk with a mixer, set aside for 10-15 minutes to enable the mixture rise.

2. next, add the olive oil, salt and 1 ¾ cups of flour to the mixture and whisk at low speed until the dough is soft and sticky. If the dough continues to stick to the bowl, add a bit more flour.

3. Remove dough from the bowl and knead into a ball on a smooth, clean and lightly floured surface.

4. Evenly oil a large bowl with olive oil, place kneaded dough in the bowl and cover for about 1-2 hours. This is to enable the dough rise and double in size.

5. Remove the dough from the bowl and knead into a flat shape about 1 inch thick on a clean and lightly floured surface. Slice the dough with a knife and divide into 8 pieces.

6. Shape each piece with your hands into small round balls, place in an oiled bowl to sit for 30 minutes.

7. After 30 minutes, place dough balls on a clean floured surface and pat with your hands to form a flat slightly round bread 1/2 inch thick, set aside to rest for 5 minutes.

8. Space out the oven racks and preheat the oven to 325F. Grease two 9 inch square baking pans with oil and set aside.

9. Divide bread into baking pans and place in the oven, bake for 5-10 minutes until the bread begins to rise and the bottom has brown spots. Flip sides and bake for 3 minutes until fully stuffed with hot air.

10. Remove from the oven and cool, if desired break bread in half and open to fill the pocket with desired stuffing.

12

YUKON POTATO, LEEK AND FETA FRITTATA

Prep Time:15 minutes
Cook Time: 35 minutes
Calories per Serving: 226
Serves: 6 yields

Ingredients

2 medium unpeeled Yukon Gold potatoes (3/4 pound)
2 tablespoons butter, unsalted
2 leeks
Salt and freshly ground black pepper
10 large eggs
1/3 cup whole milk
1 cup crumbled feta cheese

Instructions:

1. Cut the white and tender green parts of the leeks into 2, across the length and slice thinly.

2. Preheat the oven to 350F.

3. Place the potatoes in a medium saucepan, cover with water and bring to a boil. Boil 15 minutes. Drain, cool slightly, and then cut into 1/2-inches.

4. Melt the butter in a pan and then add the leeks. Cook for 4

minutes and then add the potatoes and cook 3 minutes. Add salt and pepper.

5. Whisk the eggs in a bowl, add the milk and salt and pepper and then pour over the leeks and potatoes, cook 5 minutes. Do not stir.

6. Sprinkle the feta cheese over it and then remove to the oven to bake. Bake 15 minutes. Slide and cut into wedges.

LUNCH

13

MOZZARELLA PITA MELTS

Prep Time: 5 minutes
Cook Time: 7 minutes
Total Time: 13 minutes
Calories per Serving: 380
Serves: 2

Ingredients:

1 teaspoon of olive oil
2 (6 inch) whole wheat pita
1 cup of grated mozzarella cheese
1/4 small red onion, chopped finely
1/4 cup of pitted kalamata olives, halved
2 tablespoons of fresh parsley, chopped finely

Instructions:

1. Preheat your oven to 400F, line spray a baking sheet with cooking spray.

2. Lightly brush the pita on both sides and place in the oven to warm for 2 minutes.

3. Remove from the oven and layer the warmed pita with mozzarella, onions and olives.

4. Place back to the oven and cook for 5 minutes until heated through and the cheese melted.

5. Remove from the oven and place on a plate, sprinkle with fresh parsley and serve.

14

ROASTED GRAPE AND GOAT CHEESE CROSTINI

Prep Time: 10 minutes
Cook Time: 25 minutes
Total Time: 35 minutes
Calories per Serving: 253
Serves: 10

Ingredients:
1/2 teaspoon of kosher salt
1 tablespoon of fresh rosemary, chopped
1 1/2 tablespoons of extra virgin olive oil
4 cups of red seedless grapes, stems removed
For the Crostini:
1 French baguette cut into 1/3 inch rounds
1/4 cup of olive oil
For the Goat Cheese Spread:
5 oz of goat cheese
4 oz of cream cheese
3/4 teaspoon of black pepper

Instructions
1. Preheat the oven to 350F.
2. Place the grapes, olive oil, rosemary and salt in a bowl, toss

until well coated and then arrange neatly in a rimmed baking sheet.

3. Prepare the crostini; lightly brush the bread with olive oil and place in a separate baking sheet.

4. Place both baking sheet in the oven. Bake the bread for 10-15 minutes until just golden and the grapes for 25-30 minutes until it wrinkles and release some juice, stir halfway through.

5. While the grapes roast, prepare the goat cheese spread. Combine all the ingredients in a food processor and pulse until smooth and creamy. Transfer to a bowl and set aside.

6. After the bread and grapes have been roasted, assemble the crostini: Spread toasted crostini with about 1-2 teaspoons of goat cheese spread and top with roasted grapes. Enjoy!

15

PARMESAN-CRUSTED PORK CHOPS

Prep Time: 10 minutes
    Cook Time: 16 minutes
    Total Time: 26 minutes
    Calories per Serving: 290
    Serves: 4

Ingredients:

1 egg, beaten
1 teaspoon of Dijon mustard
1 tablespoon of warm water
1/4 cup of Italian bread crumbs
1/3 cup of Parmesan cheese, finely grated
4 boneless pork loin chops, 3/4 inch thick
1 tablespoon of olive oil

Instructions:

1. Heat oven to 375F. Line a baking sheet with foil and set aside.

2. Combine the egg, mustard and water in a shallow bowl, using a separate shallow bowl, combine the bread crumbs and parmesan and mix until well combined.

3. Arrange the bowls assembly line style and dip the pork first in the egg mixture, then in the bread crumb mixture.

4. Heat olive oil in a large skillet set over medium heat. Add the pork chops and cook for about 2-3 minutes per side until golden brown. Remove from heat and transfer to the baking sheet.

5. Place the baking sheet in the oven and bake for about 10 minutes until pork is no longer pink at the center and a meat thermometer inserted in the center reads 145F.

16

PECAN-CRUSTED CATFISH

Prep Time: 10 minutes
Cook Time: 10 minutes
Total Time: 20 minutes
Calories per Serving: 341
Serves: 2

Ingredients:
2 tablespoons of Dijon mustard
1 tablespoon of 2% milk
1/4 teaspoon of dill weed
1/2 cup of ground pecans
2 6 oz. catfish fillets

Instructions:
1. Line a baking sheet with cooking spray and set aside.
2. Add the mustard, dill and milk in a shallow bowl and stir until well mixed.
3. Place ground pecans in a separate bowl and set aside.
4. Dip fillets first in the mustard mixture, then in the pecan, ensure they are well coated and place in the coated baking sheet.
5. Transfer to the oven and bake at 400F for 10-12 minutes

until the fish flakes easily with a fork. Remove from heat and set aside to cool before serving.

17

ROASTED MINI PEPPERS

Prep Time: 10 minutes
Cook Time: 20 minutes
Total Time: 30 minutes
Calories per Serving: 113
Serves: 2

Ingredients:
8 oz of mini peppers, halved & seeds removed
1 tablespoon of olive oil
1/2 teaspoon of kosher salt
1/4 teaspoon of black pepper
1/2 teaspoon of garlic powder
1/2 teaspoon of dried oregano
2 tablespoons of Parmesan, finely grated

Instructions

1. Preheat the oven to 375F and line a large rimmed baking sheet with foil.

2. Combine the mini peppers, oregano, garlic, olive oil, salt, pepper and parmesan in a shallow bowl and toss until well coated.

3. Transfer the seasoned peppers to the baking sheet, arrange

them neatly in a single layer and place in the oven to bake until tender for about 20-30 minutes. Remove from heat and serve.

18

MOROCCAN PORK KEBABS

Prep Time: 15 minutes
Cook Time: 40 minutes
Total Time: 55 minutes
Calories per Serving: 375
Serves: 4

Ingredients:
1/4 cup of orange juice
4 tablespoons of olive oil
1 tablespoon of ground cumin
1 tablespoon of tomato paste
3/4 teaspoon of black pepper
1 1/2 teaspoons of kosher salt
1/8 teaspoon of ground cinnamon
1 clove of garlic, finely chopped
1 small red onion, cut into 8 wedges
1 small of eggplant, unpeeled, cut into 1-inch chunks
1 1/2 pounds of boneless pork loin, cut into 1 1/2-inch chunks
Pita bread, for serving
1/2 pint of cucumber-yogurt sauce

1/2 small cucumber, thinly sliced

2 tablespoons chopped fresh mint wooden skewers, soaked for 30 minutes

Instructions:

1. Preheat the oven to 375 F and line a baking tray with foil.

2. Add the tomato paste, garlic, orange juice and cumin, 2 tablespoons of olive oil, 1 teaspoon of salt and 1/2 teaspoon of pepper. Whisk until well combined.

3. Add the pork, toss to coat well and afterwards cover with aluminum foil then place in the fridge to marinate for at least an hour.

4. While the pork marinates, combine the eggplant, onion, salt, pepper and the remaining 2 tablespoons of oil in a bowl and stir until well coated. Arrange the onions and eggplant on wooden skewers.

5. Transfer the skewers to the baking tray and bake for 15-20 minutes turning the skewers regularly.

6. Place the pork over the skewer and bake for 20-25 minutes until the pork is tender and the vegetables cooked through.

7. During the last 5 minutes, loosely wrap the bread in foil and place over the pork. Remove from heat and set aside to cool for a few minutes.

8. Divide the skewers and bread to individual plates and serve with yoghurt sauce, mint and cucumber.

19

HERB BAKED CHICKEN TENDERS

Prep Time: 60 minutes
   Cook Time: 20 minutes
   Total Time: 80 minutes
   Serves: 4

Ingredients:

1 1/5 lb. of chicken tenders

6 fresh sprigs

1/4 cup of fresh Italian parsley, washed, chopped, plus more for serving

1/2 cup of olive oil

2 tablespoons of balsamic vinegar

1 teaspoon of salt

1/2 teaspoon of fresh ground pepper medley

1 teaspoon of minced garlic

Instructions:

1. Add all ingredients except the chicken tenders in a bowl and mix until well combined.

2. Add the chicken, toss to coat well and afterwards cover with aluminum foil then place in the fridge to marinate for at least an hour.

3. Preheat the oven to 400F, and when the chicken is done marinating, drain marinade and transfer to the lower rack of the oven to bake for 20 minutes turning halfway through.

4. Check doneness by inserting a thermometer in the chicken, the temperature should read 165F.

20

HEALTHY OVEN ROASTED POTATOES

Prep Time: 10 minutes
Cook Time: 20 minutes
Total Time: 30 minutes
Calories per Serving: 319
Serves: 4

Ingredients:

½ teaspoon salt
1 tablespoon of olive oil
1 tablespoon of minced garlic
½ teaspoon of red pepper flakes
4 large potatoes, peeled and cubed
1 tablespoon of fresh parsley, chopped
1 tablespoon of fresh rosemary, chopped
1 tablespoon of fresh basil, finely chopped

Instructions:

1. Preheat the oven to 400F
2. Combine all ingredients in a bowl and toss until well mixed.
3. Transfer potatoes to a baking sheet and place in the preheated oven to roast for 20-25 minutes until evenly browned on all sides, turn occasionally.

21

HONEY BALSAMIC CHICKEN BREASTS AND VEGGIES

Prep Time: 60 minutes
Cook Time: 30 minutes
Total Time: 90 minutes
Calories per Serving: 411
Serves: 4

Ingredients:
1 lb. asparagus, trimmed
2 cups of cherry tomatoes
16 oz of baby red potatoes, quartered
2 tablespoons of extra virgin olive oil
Kosher salt and freshly ground black pepper, to taste
2 tablespoons of fresh parsley leaves, finely chopped
For the chicken:
2 tablespoons of honey
1/2 teaspoon dried basil
1/4 cup of balsamic vinegar
2 cloves of garlic, minced
1 tablespoon of Dijon mustard
1/2 teaspoon of dried oregano
4 chicken breasts, boneless & skinless

Kosher salt and freshly ground black pepper, to taste

Instructions:

1. Prepare the chicken: add all ingredients except the chicken breasts into a bowl and mix until well combined.

2. Next add the chicken, toss to coat and afterwards cover with aluminum foil. Place in the fridge to marinate for at least an hour. After an hour, drain marinade and set aside.

3. Preheat the oven to 375F; lightly coat a baking sheet with non stick cooking spray.

4. Arrange potatoes and tomatoes neatly in a single layer in the baking sheet, lightly top with olive oil and a sprinkle of salt and pepper to taste.

5. Place chicken in the baking sheet beside the tomatoes, transfer baking sheet to the oven and roast for about 20-25 minutes until completely cooked through. During the last 10 minutes of cooking time, stir in asparagus.

6. When chicken has completely cooked through, remove from heat and serve garnished with parsley.

22

BAKED GARLIC FRIES

Prep Time:10 minutes
Cook Time: 25 minutes
Total Time: 35 minutes
Calories per Serving: 454
Serves: 3

Ingredients:

1/2 teaspoon of salt
3 tablespoons of avocado oil
2 tablespoons of garlic, minced
3 tablespoons of minced parsley
1.5 lbs russet potatoes, sliced into 1/4" thick sticks

Instructions:

1. Preheat the oven to 400F.

2. Heat the oil in a saucepan set over low heat, add the garlic and sauté for 5 minutes. Remove from heat and strain garlic from the oil.

3. Place the oil in a rimmed baking sheet, add potato sticks, salt and stir with your hands until thoroughly coated.

4. Arrange the fries in a single layer and transfer to the oven

bake for 15-20 minutes until the bottoms start to turn slightly golden then flip sides and continue cooking until evenly golden for about 5 minutes.

23

TOMATO AVOCADO MELT

Prep Time: 5 minutes

Cook Time: 5 minutes

Total Time: 10 minutes

Calories per Serving: 635

Serves: 2

Ingredients:

4 slices of bread

A pinch of cayenne pepper

2 tablespoons of mayonnaise

1 small tomato, chopped finely

1/2 medium avocado, chopped finely

8 slices of cheddar cheese

Instructions:

1. Preheat oven to 350F and line a baking sheet with cooking spray.

2. Spread mayonnaise over the bread and sprinkle with cayenne pepper.

3. Top with avocado, tomatoes and cheese and a layer of bread.

4. Transfer to the baking sheet and heat for about 5 minutes until the cheese is melted and bread is slightly toasted.

24

ROASTED-FENNEL DITALINI AND SHRIMP

Prep Time: 10 minutes
Cook Time: 40 minutes
Total Time: 50 minutes
Calories per Serving: 420
Serves: 4

Ingredients:

1 lb. fresh large shrimp
1 teaspoon of fennel seeds
1 teaspoon of salt, divided
4 cloves of garlic, finely chopped
1/2 lb of whole wheat ditalini pasta
2 tablespoons of extra virgin olive oil
1 fennel bulb, halved and sliced crosswise
1/2 teaspoon of freshly ground black pepper

Instructions:

1. First preheat the oven to 400F.

2. Place the fennel seeds in a saucepan set over medium heat and toast for about 5 minutes, afterwards add shrimp, water, and 1/2 teaspoon of salt and bring to a boil. Reduce heat to low and simmer for 20 minutes. Stir regularly.

3. Combine the fennel bulbs, olive oil, garlic, salt and pepper in a roasting pan, place in the oven and roast for 15 minutes, add shrimp and roast for an additional 5 minutes.

4. While it roasts, cook the pasta per package instructions, drain with a colander and set aside.

5. After shrimp is cooked, remove from the roasting pan and add pasta, roast for another 5 minutes. Remove from heat and set aside.

PORK, BEEF AND LAMB

25

BAKED HAM AND CHEESE ROLLUPS

Prep Time: 10 minutes
Cook Time: 25 minutes
Total Time: 35 minutes
Serves: 12

Ingredients:

1/2 cup of butter melted
1 tablespoon of poppy seeds
1 tube crescent dough sheet
1 1/2 tablespoons of yellow mustard
1 tablespoons of dried minced onion
1/2 teaspoons of Worcestershire sauce
3/4 lb. Black Forest Ham, sliced thinly
12 slices of Swiss cheese, sliced thinly

Instructions:

1. Preheat oven to 350F and lightly coat a 9x13 inch baking dish with cooking spray, set aside.

2. Roll the crescent dough on a clean flat surface and shape into a 13x18 inch rectangle, use a sheet pan of similar size to measure if necessary. Top with the sliced ham and cheese.

3. Roll the dough tightly and cut into 12 pieces. Transfer to the prepared baking dish and arrange neatly, evenly spaced.

4. Next, combine the seasoning ingredients in a bowl, stir to mix well. Spread the sauce evenly over the rollups.

5. Place in the oven and bake for about 20-25 minutes until lightly browned. Remove from heat and set aside to cool before serving.

26

PORK ROLLS WITH TERIYAKI SAUCE

Prep Time: 10 minutes
Cook Time: 15 minutes
Total Time: 25 minutes
Calories per Serving:
Serves: 6 rolls

Ingredients:

6 pork cutlets
15-18 green beans, ends trimmed
2 tablespoons of vegetable oil
1 carrot, sliced into 15-18 thin strips
1 red bell pepper, seeded and thinly sliced
All purpose flour
Salt and pepper to taste
For the Sauce:
1 tablespoon of sugar
2 tablespoons of soy sauce
2 tablespoons of warm water

Instructions:

1. Place a few cups of salted water in a saucepan and bring to a boil. Add the vegetables and boil for 3-5 minutes.

2. Next, remove from heat, strain and pat dry with a paper towel.

3. Prepare the sauce: Combine sauce ingredients in a small bowl, set aside.

4. To prepare the pork cutlet, dust a clean, flat surface with flour, roll pork cutlet on the surface and top each one with 3 green beans, carrots and peppers each.

5. Season with salt and pepper and roll the pork tightly. Secure rolled pork with toothpick and set aside.

6. Next, heat olive oil in a saucepan set over medium-low heat. Add the pork rolls and cook for 8-10 minutes until golden brown. Stir regularly to ensure it is evenly cooked.

7. Stir in prepared sauce and cook for 2-3 minutes. Remove from heat and set aside to cool before serving alone or with vegetables.

27

KETO PORK CHOPS PARMESAN BREADING

Prep Time: 15 minutes
Cook Time: 12 minutes
Total Time: 27 minutes
Calories per Serving: 370
Serves: 4

Ingredients:

¼ teaspoon of salt
½ teaspoons of garlic powder
¼ teaspoon of ground white pepper
4 boneless pork chops
1 large egg, beaten
4 oz of shredded parmesan
2 tablespoons of extra virgin olive

Instructions:

1. Preheat the oven to 350F. Add the first 3 ingredients into a bowl and stir to combine.

2. Sprinkle the garlic mixture over the pork; press with your hands to ensure seasoning seep through.

3. Next, place parmesan, egg in a separate plate and arrange assembly line style.

4. Dip pork chops first in the egg, then the cheese, ensure both sides are well coated and set aside.

5. Place the pork in a baking dish and cook each side for about 5 minutes until golden brown and crusty.

6. Remove from heat and serve alone or with preferred side dish.

28

PULLED PORK CARNITAS QUESADILLAS

Prep Time: 15 minutes
Cook Time: 20 minutes
Total Time: 35 minutes
Calories per Serving: 504
Serves: 4

Ingredients:
1 1/2 cups of shredded Mexican pulled pork, carnitas
1 1/2 cups shredded mozzarella cheese
8 tortillas
1/2 cup corn kernels
1/2 cup diced red bell pepper
1 tablespoon of olive oil
Salt and pepper
Fresh parsley or coriander, finely chopped (optional garnish)
For the caramelized onions:
1 1/2 tablespoon of butter
2 brown onions, halved and finely sliced
1 1/2 tablespoon of brown sugar
1 tablespoon of balsamic vinegar
1/2 teaspoon of salt

Black pepper

Instructions:

1. To prepare the Caramelized Onions: Heat butter in a saucepan set over low heat, add onions and cook until slightly brown, stir regularly.

2. Add the rest of the onions ingredients and cook for an additional 5 minutes until caramelized. Remove from heat and set aside to cool.

3. Next, heat 1/2 tablespoon of oil in a separate skillet set over high heat, add carnitas and press down tightly with a spatula until heated through and the bottom is golden brown. This takes about 2-3 minutes, remove from heat and set aside.

4. For the tortillas; lay out the tortillas, spread cheese evenly across half of the tortillas, top with carnitas, capsicum, onions and corn. Add salt and pepper then fold in half.

5. To cook, preheat the oven to 350F; lightly coat a baking dish with cooking spray.

6. Arrange quesadillas neatly in the pan and cook until slightly browned at the bottom, flip sides and cook until the other half is evenly browned. Remove from heat and serve immediately.

29

CRISPY PORK WONTONS

Prep Time: 40 minutes
　　Cook Time: 30 minutes
　　Total Time: 70 minutes
　　Calories Per Serving: 50 (per wantons)
　　Serves: 50 wantons
Ingredients:
50 wonton wrappers
1 lb. ground pork
2 large eggs, beaten
1/2 teaspoon of sea salt
1/4 cup of low-sodium soy sauce
1 cup of carrots, finely grated
3 cloves of fresh garlic, minced
1 tablespoon of ground black pepper
1 cup of yellow onion, finely chopped
1 quart of canola oil, for frying
Instructions:
　　1. Add the carrots, pork, soy sauce, onions, salt and pepper in a large bowl and mix until well combined.
　　2. Lay the wonton wrappers on a smooth, clean surface.

Spoon a teaspoon of filling into the center of each wrapper, lightly brush the edges with the egg and fold the wrapper to form a triangle. Press the edges and the corners leading up to the center to seal.

3. Ensure wrappers are not overfilled. This prevents them from breaking when it comes in contact with heat.

4. Preheat your oven to 350F, add oil to a large baking sheet and set aside

5. After the oven is preheated, working in batches, space wontons in prepared baking sheet and transfer to the oven.

6. Fry until golden brown, afterwards remove from heat and repeat in batches until completed.

7. Remove from heat and place in a bowl lined in paper towel to absorb the oil. Serve with preferred dipping sauce.

8. Helpful tip: wrap and fry a small amount then taste to check flavor and adjust seasoning as desired.

30

TUSCAN PORK CHOPS

Prep Time: 10 minutes
Cook Time: 20 minutes
Total Time: 30 minutes
Serves: 4

Ingredients:

1/4 cup of flour
1 teaspoon of salt
3/4 teaspoon of pepper
4 cloves of garlic, minced
1/3 cup of balsamic vinegar
3 plum tomatoes, seeded and diced
4 boneless pork chops, 1 inch thick
1 tablespoon of extra virgin olive oil
1/3 cup of chicken broth, low sodium
2 tablespoons of capers
Fresh parsley

Instructions:

1. Preheat the oven to 350F, line a baking sheet with cooking spray and set aside.

2. Combine the flour, salt and pepper in a large bowl and add pork chops to the mixture, stirring until well coated.

3. Place pork chop in the prepared baking sheet and cook for 3-5 minutes per side until evenly golden brown.

4. Meanwhile, heat olive oil in a skillet set over low heat, add garlic and sauté for about 1-2 minutes.

5. Next, increase heat to medium. Stir in the vinegar, chicken broth, tomatoes, capers and pork chops and bring the sauce to a boil.

6. Reduce heat to low and simmer for 5-7 minutes until pork is done. Remove from heat and serve with tomatoes mixture and a sprinkle of parsley. Enjoy!

31

PARMESAN BAKED PORK CHOPS

Prep Time: 10 minutes
  Cook Time: 40 minutes
  Total Time: 50 minutes
  Serves: 4

Ingredients:

1 tablespoon of olive oil
1 teaspoon of garlic powder
1 cup of Italian bread crumbs
1 cup of shredded parmesan cheese
4 boneless pork chops, 1/2 inch thick
1 teaspoon of freshly ground black pepper

Instructions:

1. Combine the cheese, bread crumbs, pepper and garlic powder in a large mixing bowl.

2. Next, brush the pork chops with olive oil then dip on all sides in the cheese mixture.

3. Place the pork chops in a baking sheet and transfer to the oven to bake at 350F for 30-40 minutes.

32

PORK SATAY WITH PEANUT DIPPING SAUCE

Prep Time: 2 hours
Cook Time: 20 minutes
Calories Per Serving: 64 (per skewer)
Serves: 18

Ingredients:

2 garlic cloves, minced
1/4 cup chopped green onions
1/4 cup soy sauce
1 tablespoon fresh lime juice
2 tablespoons of brown sugar
1 (1 lbs.) pork tenderloin, trimmed & halved
1 tablespoon creamy peanut butter
18 (6-inch) wooden skewers
For the Peanut Sauce:
1 teaspoon of soy sauce
1 clove of garlic, minced
1 teaspoon of ginger, minced
2 teaspoons of fresh lime juice
1/3 cup of less-sodium chicken broth
1/4 cup reduced-fat creamy peanut butter

Instructions:

1. Wrap pork in a plastic bag and pound with a meat mallet until 1/4 inch thick, cut further into 1 inch skewer sized strips. Place strips in a jar with a sealable lid and set aside.

2. Combine the rest of the ingredients except the skewers into a bowl and stir until well mixed, transfer mixture to the jar. Close the lid and shake until well coated. Place in the refrigerator to marinate for at least 2 hours. While pork marinates, soak skewers in warm water.

3. Preheat oven broiler and prepare the peanut dipping sauce: combine all ingredients then place in a saucepan set over low heat. Simmer for 5-10 minutes until heated and slightly thick, remove from heat.

4. Remove tenderloin and drain marinade, thread tenderloin onto each skewer and place on a broiler rack. Coat with cooking spray then transfer to the oven to broil for about 3-5 minutes on each side until done.

5. Serve pork skewers with dipping sauce, enjoy!

33

VIETNAMESE CARAMEL PORK

Prep Time: 10 minutes
Cook Time: 1 hour
Total Time: 1 hour 10 minutes
Calories per Serving: 437
Serves: 4

Ingredients:

1/2 cup of brown sugar
1 tablespoon of warm water
2 cloves of garlic, minced
1 1/4 cups of coconut water
1/4 teaspoon of white pepper
1 1/2 tablespoon of fish sauce
1 shallot, finely sliced
2 lb pork shoulder cut into 1 inch pieces
1 1/4 cups of onions, finely chopped
Red chili and shallots, to garnish

Instructions:

1. Heat the sugar and water in a large saucepan set over medium heat. Cook until the mixture bubbles and the sugar is melted,

2. Reduce heat to low and stir in the rest of the ingredients, simmer uncovered for about an hour, stir regularly. Continue to cook until the liquid is gone and only the fat remains.

3. Remove from heat and set aside to cool, serve with rice topped with red chilli and shallots.

34

BEEF TACO EGG ROLLS

Prep Time: 10 minutes
Cook Time: 12 minutes
Total Time: 22 minutes
Calories per Serving: 340
Serves: 8

Ingredients:

1 lb. lean ground beef
1 teaspoon of cilantro
1 tablespoon of olive oil
2 cloves of garlic, chopped
1/2 packet of taco seasoning
1 cup of shredded Mexican cheese
1/2 medium onion, finely chopped
1/2 can of cilantro lime rotel tomatoes
16 egg roll wrappers

Instructions:

1. Preheat the oven to 400F
2. Heat oil in a skillet set over low-medium heat, add onions, garlic and sauté until fragrant.
3. Next, add the taco seasoning, beef, cilantro rotel, salt and

pepper and cook until the beef is broken into tiny pieces, stir regularly.

4. Lay out egg wrappers on a clean surface and brush with warm water, fill wrappers with beef filling and cheese then gently fold diagonally to close. Brush the edges with water and fold.

5. Place the wrappers in a baking tray, coat with cooking spray and place in the middle shelf of the oven. Cook for 15 minutes, flip sides halfway through cooking.

6. Remove from heat and serve sprinkled with cilantro.

35

TASTY BEEF STROGANOFF CASSEROLE

Prep Time: 15 minutes
Cook Time: 2 hours 15 minutes
Total Time: 2 hours 30 minutes
Calories per Serving: 332
Serves: 8

Ingredients:

1/2 teaspoon of salt
1/2 teaspoon of pepper
1/2 teaspoon of paprika
1/3 cup of all purpose flour
1/2 teaspoon of garlic powder
2 tablespoons of butter, room temperature
2/3 cup of low sodium beef broth
3-4 sprigs of fresh thyme
2 tablespoons of olive oil
1 1/2 lb of stewing beef
1 1/2 cups of mushrooms, halved
1 large onion, finely chopped
8 oz of dry egg noodles
1 tablespoon of fresh parsley

For the crumb topping:
1/2 cup of panko bread crumbs
1 tablespoon of fresh parsley
1/2 teaspoon of garlic powder
1 1/2 tablespoons of melted butter
For the sauce:
1/2 cup of sour cream
2 teaspoons of cornstarch
1 carton of beef flavor (preferably McCormick Simply Better Gravy)

Instructions

1. Preheat oven to 300F, Line a 9 x 13 inch pan with cooking spray and set aside.

2. Combine the first 5 ingredients in a large mixing bowl, add beef and toss until well coated.

3. Heat the olive oil and butter in a skillet set over medium heat, add beef chunks and cook until browned and crusty all over. Remove from heat.

4. Prepare the crumb topping: combine all ingredients into a bowl.

4. Place the onions, mushrooms beef, thyme and beef broth in the baking dish, top with crumb topping. Tent with aluminum foil and place in the oven to bake for 1 hour 30 minutes until tender.

5. While it bakes, prepare the sauce: combine all ingredients in a bowl and set aside covered.

6. Prepare the egg noodles following the package instructions, drain and set aside.

7. After the beef is cooked and tender, remove beef and thyme sprigs from the baking pan. Stir in the egg noodles and the sauce and bake for an additional 10-15 minutes until bubbly.

36

TEXAS OVEN-ROASTED BEEF BRISKET

Prep Time: 15 minutes
Cook Time: 3 hours
Serves: 10

Ingredients:

1 bay leaf, crushed
1 tablespoon of sugar
2 tablespoons of salt
1 1/2 cups of beef stock
2 teaspoons of dry mustard
2 tablespoons of chili powder
1 tablespoon of garlic powder
1 tablespoon of onion powder
1 tablespoon of ground black pepper
4 pounds of beef brisket, trimmed

Instructions:

1. Preheat the oven to 325F, line a roasting pan with cooking spray and set aside.

2. Combine the chili and onion powders, salt, pepper, garlic, mustard and bay leave in a bowl. Place the raw brisket in the bowl and season on both sides.

3. Transfer brisket to the roasting pan and roast for an hour, afterwards remove from heat.

4. Add beef stock and warm water to the pan until there is about 1/2 an inch of liquid in the pan. Cover and return to the oven.

5. Reduce heat to 300F and continue cooking for about 2 hours until brisket is fork tender.

6. Remove from heat, trim the fat away from brisket and slice thinly across the grain, serve with juice from the pan.

37

BAKED STEAK WITHPARMESAN AND PEPPER CRUST

Prep Time: 5 minutes

Cook Time: 15 minutes

Total Time: 20 minutes

Calories per Serving: 280

Serves: 6

Ingredients:

6 beef sirloin steaks

1 tablespoon of olive oil

1/3 cup of parmesan cheese, grated

1 teaspoon of cracked black pepper

Instructions:

1. Heat oven to 350F

2. Heat oil in a large oven proof skillet set over medium heat, add steaks and cook each side for about 3 minutes. Remove from heat and top with cheese and pepper.

3. Transfer the skillet to the oven and bake for about 10 minutes until a thermometer inserted in the center of the steak reads 160F.

38

SIMPLE STEAK

Prep Time: 5minutes
Cook Time: 15 minutes
Total Time: 20 minutes
Serves: 2
Ingredients:
1/2 lb. quality cut steak
Salt and freshly ground black pepper
Instructions
1. Preheat the oven to 390F
2. Place steak in a bowl and coat with salt and pepper.
2. Transfer to the baking pan and cook for 12-15 minutes until crispy.

39

CORNED BEEF EGG ROLLS

Prep Time: 10 minutes
Cook Time: 18 minutes
Total Time: 28 minutes
Serves: 8

Ingredients:

8 egg roll wrappers
1 tablespoon of butter
2 cloves of garlic, minced
1 cup of hash brown potatoes
1 medium onion, finely chopped
1 cup of cabbage, finely chopped
2 tablespoons of Dijon mustard
1 cup of cooked corned beef, finely chopped
A pinch of salt
Freshly ground black pepper
2 tablespoons of olive oil
Thousand island salad dressing, to garnish

Instructions:

1. Melt the butter in a skillet set over medium heat, add onions and garlic and sauté for about 4 minutes.

2. Next, add the cabbage and cook for 3 minutes stirring regularly.

3. Add potatoes and cook for about 5-7 minutes until the potatoes and cabbage are tender, stir regularly. Afterwards add the corned beef, mustard and stir for w2 minutes before removing from heat.

4. Transfer to a heat proof bowl, season with salt and pepper and set aside to cool.

5. Preheat the oven to 375F.

6. Place the egg roll wrappers on a clean, flat surface. Gently add about a tablespoon of filling mixture into each wrapper, brush the edges of the wrapper with water and fold in the corners over the filling.

7. Remember not to seal filling too tightly.

8. Transfer wrappers to a baking sheet and coat with cooking spray, place in the oven to cook for 15-18 minutes until crisp and golden brown. Remove from heat and serve with dressing.

40

THIN-SLICED BREADED TOP ROUND CUTLETS

Prep Time: 10minutes
Cook Time: 10 minutes
Total Time: 20 minutes
Serves: 4

Ingredients:

3 eggs, beaten
2 cups of breadcrumbs
1 cup of all purpose flour
2 cloves of garlic, minced
2 teaspoons of salt, divided
1 teaspoon of ground pepper, divided
1-1 1/2 pounds beef steaks, thinly sliced

Instructions:

1. Preheat the oven to 350F.

2. Wrap steaks in a clean bag and pound with a meat mallet to create a uniform 1/8-inch thick cutlets.

3. Place breadcrumbs in a bowl, then the eggs and garlic in another bowl. Season the steak with salt and pepper then dredge in the eggs mixture, then in the breadcrumbs.

4. Place in a baking pan and lightly coat with cooking spray.

5. Bake for 3-5 minutes per side until golden brown, afterwards remove from the oven and set on a cooling rack to cool before serving.

41

TASTY GARLIC AND ORANGE JUICE STEAK

Prep Time: 5minutes

Cook Time: 60 minutes

Total Time: 65 minutes

Calories per Serving: 556

Serves: 4

Ingredients:

1/4 cup of orange juice

1 teaspoon of ground cumin

2 tablespoons of lime juice

2 tablespoons of olive oil

4 cloves of minced garlic

Salt and pepper to taste

2 lb. skirt steak, fat trimmed

Instructions:

1. Combine all ingredients in a large mixing bowl, add the steak and marinate in the fridge for at least 2 hours or overnight.

2. Preheat the oven to 390F.

3. Remove from the fridge and reserve marinade mixture, place steak in the grill pan and transfer to the oven.

4. Grill in batches flipping beef every 5-8 minutes until crisp for even grilling.

5. While it grills, place reserved marinade in a saucepan and cook over low heat until the sauce thickens.

6. Serve grilled beef with sauce, enjoy.

42

LAMB SHANKS WITH OLIVES AND CAPERS

Prep Time: 30 minutes

Cook Time: 4 hours

Calories per Serving: 408

Serves: 4

Ingredients

6 lamb shanks (lb. each)

1 jar (4 oz.) capers

1 1/2 cups pitted green olives in brine (Picholine)

3 tablespoons dried rosemary or 1/4 cup fresh rosemary leaves

1 bottle (750 ml.) dry white wine

2 teaspoons freshly ground pepper

3 tablespoons lemon juice

2 teaspoons grated lemon peel

Lemon Couscous

About 3 cups watercress sprigs, rinsed and crisped

Instructions:

1. Rinse lamb, pat dry and lay shanks side by side in a pan. Bake in a 450F for 25 minutes, turning halfway, until completely browned.

Pork, Beef And Lamb

2. Pass capers and olive through a strainer. Rinse and drain. Add rosemary to a blender and blend with 1 cup of the wine.

3. Scatter the capers and olives, over lamb and pour the rosemary-wine mix over lamb evenly. Add the remaining wine and stir to scrape browned bitsup. Sprinkle pepper and lemon peel over it; add the lemon juice to pan andcover tightly with foil.

4. Reduce oven temperature to 325F. Bake for 3 hours until meat is very tender and pulls easily from bone.

5. Spoon lemon couscous evenly into wide bowls. Lift lamb shanks from pan with tongs and set on couscous in each bowl. Skim fat from juices in panand discard. Ladle juices with olives and capers. Garnish with about 1/2 cup watercress sprigs.

CHICKEN AND TURKEY

43

JERK-SPICED TURKEY LOAF

Prep Time: 15 minutes
Cook Time: 60 minutes
Calories per Serving: 219
Serves: 8

Ingredients

8 oz. mushrooms
1 onion (8 oz.)
2 tablespoons vegetable oil
1/2 teaspoon salt
1/2 teaspoon ground allspice
1/2 teaspoon ground nutmeg
1/4 teaspoon cayenne
1/4 teaspoon ground cinnamon
3 tablespoons white vinegar
2 tablespoons molasses
1/2 cup all-purpose flour
1 1/2 lb. ground breast turkey
1/2 cup low-fat chicken broth
1 egg
3/4 cup pickled cocktail onions, drained &each cut in half

6 oz. thinly sliced prosciutto

Instructions:

1. Rinse mushrooms, drain, and chop finely. Peel and chop onions finely. Add both to pan and cook in oil for about 7 minutes until browned.

2. Add salt, allspice, nutmeg, cayenne and cinnamon. Stir about 2 minutes until fragrant. Stir in vinegar and molasses. Scrape into a large bowl. Add the flour to the bowl and mix to blend, stir repeatedly until about 5 minutes until lukewarm.

3. Add the turkey, the broth, and egg; mix well. Add the pickled onions and gently stir.

4. In a single layer, place the prosciutto slices in a greased pan, slightly overlapping edges. Scrape the meat mixture into the pan, gently spreading out to level. Neatly fold ends of the prosciutto slices over the meat.

5. Bake turkey loaf in a 350F for 50 minutes. Insert a thermometer to ensure it attains 160F. Let stand 15 minutes. Invert a larger, rimmed platter over the pan; both together and invert. Lift off pan to release loaf.

44

RICOTTA AND PARSLEY ROLLED TURKEY BREASTS

Prep Time: 15 minutes
Cook Time: 25 minutes
Serves: 4

Ingredients:

1 egg, beaten
1 teaspoon of paprika
Crushed tortilla chips
1 cup of ricotta cheese
1 turkey breast, quartered
1 teaspoon of garlic powder
1/4 cup of Italian parsley, chopped
Salt and ground black pepper, to taste

Instructions:

1. Preheat the oven to 350F.

2. Flatten each piece of turkey with a rolling pin and set aside.

3. Add the ricotta cheese, garlic, parsley and cumin powder in a bowl, set aside.

4. Next, combine the egg and paprika in another bowl, in a third bowl combine the salt, pepper and tortilla chips.

5. Scoop the parsley mixture in the middle of each turkey breast and roll them up.

6. Dip turkey rolls first in the egg then in the tortilla chip mixture, ensure they are well coated. Transfer rolls in batches if necessary to a baking sheet and coat with cooking spray.

7. Place in the oven and cook for 25 minutes, repeat with the remaining rolled up turkey.

45

SWEET AND SOUR CHICKEN

Prep Time: 15 minutes
Cook Time: 28 minutes
Total Time: 43 minutes
Serves: 3

Ingredients:

3 chicken breasts, cubed
1/2 cup of all purpose flour
1/2 cup of cornstarch
2 medium red peppers, sliced
1 onion, finely chopped
2 carrots, julienne
3/4 cups of sugar
2 tablespoons of cornstarch
1/3 cup of vinegar
2/3 cups of warm water
1/4 cup of soy sauce
1 tablespoon of ketchup

Instructions:

1. Preheat the oven to 375F. Line a baking tray with cooking spray.

2. Combine the flour, chicken and cornstarch in a large mixing bowl and stir until well combined. Shake off excess flour from the chicken and place in the baking spray.

3. Transfer chicken to the oven and bake for 20 minutes.

4. Meanwhile, add the water, sugar, soy sauce, vinegar and ketchup in a saucepan set over medium heat and bring to a boil.

5. After cooking the chicken, add the sauce mixture and the vegetables to the baking tray and cook for 5-7 minutes. Remove from heat and serve with rice. Enjoy!

46

HONEY AND WINE CHICKEN BREAST

Prep Time: 10 minutes
Cook Time: 20 minutes
Total Time: 30 minutes
Calories per Serving: 189
Serves: 4

Ingredients:

2 chicken breasts, halved
1 teaspoon of paprika
1 tablespoon of honey
3/4 teaspoon of salt
1 teaspoon of dried rosemary
1 tablespoon of butter, melted
2 tablespoons of dry white wine
1/2 teaspoon of freshly ground pepper

Instructions:

1. Preheat the oven to 330F.

2. Combine all ingredients except the butter and chicken to a bowl and stir to whisk well.

3. Coat the chicken with melted butter then place in the bowl and toss to coat with the remaining ingredients.

4. Place in the oven and bake for 15 minutes. Remove from heat and set aside to cool before serving.

47

TASTY PERU CHICKEN BBQ

Prep Time: 2 hours
Cook Time: 40 minutes
Total Time: 2 hours, 40 minutes
Calories per Serving: 377
Serves: 4

Ingredients:

1/3 cup of soy sauce
1 teaspoon of paprika
2 teaspoons of ground cumin
4 cloves of garlic, minced
2 1/2 lb. chicken, quartered
1/2 teaspoon of dried oregano
2 tablespoons of fresh lime juice

Instructions:

1. Combine all ingredients in a sealable bag, shake vigorously and marinate in the fridge for at least 2 hours.

2. Preheat the oven to 390F; drain the chicken of marinade mixture.

3. Place chicken over the grill pan and grill for 40 minutes, flip chicken every 10 minutes for even grilling.

48

TASTY ASIAN CHICKEN WINGS

Prep Time: 10 minutes
Cook Time: 25 minutes
Total Time: 35 minutes
Calories per Serving: 358
Serves: 8

Ingredients:

2 lb. chicken wings
3 teaspoons of sesame seeds
1 teaspoon of salt and pepper, each
For the Sauce:
2 packets of splenda
1 teaspoon of agave nectar
1 tablespoon of mayonnaise
1 tablespoon of sesame oil
1 tablespoon of garlic, minced
1 tablespoon of ginger, minced
2 tablespoon of red chili paste

Instructions:

1. Preheat the oven to 350F, line a small baking pan with parchment paper and set aside.

2. Place the chicken wings in a bowl and season with salt and pepper.

3. Place chicken in the baking pan, then transfer to the oven. Reduce heat to 160F and bake for 20 minutes turning chicken halfway through.

4. Meanwhile, add all the sauce ingredients in a bowl and stir to mix well.

5. Transfer chicken from the oven to a bowl, add half of the sauce mixture then toss to coat.

6. Place coated chicken back in the oven and cook for 5-10 minutes until crisp and a kitchen thermometer reads 165F.

7. Remove from heat and serve with a sprinkle of sesame seeds and extra sauce for dipping.

49

TASTY ALMOND BATTERED CHICKEN

Prep Time: 10 minutes
Cook Time: 30 minutes
Total Time: 40 minutes
Calories per Serving: 590
Serves: 4

Ingredients:

1 egg, beaten
4 medium chicken thighs
1/4 cup of coconut milk
1/2 cup of almond flour
Salt and pepper to taste
1 1/2 tablespoons of Cajun seasoning

Instructions:

1. Preheat the oven to 350F; line a baking sheet with cooking spray.

2. Combine the egg and coconut milk in a mixing bowl, combine the almond flour, Cajun seasoning, salt and pepper in a separate bowl.

3. Arrange the bowls assembly line style, dredge the chicken first in the egg mixture, then in the almond flour mixture.

4. Place the chicken in the baking sheet and cook for 30 minutes.

50

GARLIC BREADED CHICKEN BAKE

Prep Time: 10 minutes

Cook Time: 25 minutes

Calories per Serving: 311

Serves: 2

Ingredients:

1/4 cup of flour

1/4 cup of flax egg

1/2 teaspoon of salt

1/4 teaspoon of pepper

2 cloves of garlic, minced

1/4 cup of grated parmesan

1/4 cup of panko breadcrumbs

1 tablespoon of melted butter

1 large tomato, seeded and chopped

1 1/2 tablespoons of fresh basil, minced

1/2 tablespoons of extra virgin olive oil

2 (4 oz) chicken breasts, boneless & skinless

Instructions:

1. Preheat the oven to 390F. Lightly grease a baking sheet with cooking spray and set aside.

2. Combine the butter, breadcrumbs and parmesan in a small bowl, then place the flax egg and the flour in separate bowls.

3. Dredge the chicken first in flour, then the egg, then flour. Generously sprinkle the breadcrumb mixture over the chicken then place in the baking sheet. Cover with foil.

4. Place in the oven and cook for 20 minutes.

5. Meanwhile, combine the remaining ingredients in a large mixing bowl.

6. After the chicken is cooked, top with the remaining ingredients then cook for 5-8 minutes. Enjoy!

51

CRUSTED CHICKEN TENDERS

Prep Time: 10 minutes
Cook Time: 15 minutes
Serves: 3

Ingredients:

2 eggs, beaten
1/2 cup of flour
3/4 lb of chicken tenders
2 tablespoons of olive oil
1/2 cup of seasoned breadcrumbs
Salt and freshly ground black pepper

Instructions:

1. Preheat the oven to 330F.

2. Place the flour in a shallow bowl, in a separate bowl add the eggs. Combine the olive oil, breadcrumbs, salt and pepper in a third bowl and set aside.

3. Arrange the bowls assembly line style, coat the chicken in flour, then eggs and finally bread crumbs then place in the baking sheet.

4. Place in the oven and cook for 10 minutes. Flip sides, increase heat to 370F and cook for an additional 5 minutes.

52

BUFFALO CHICKEN WINGS

Prep Time: 10 minutes
Cook Time: 30 minutes
Total Time: 40 minutes
Calories per Serving: 400
Serves: 8

Ingredients:

1 teaspoon of salt
1/2 cup of butter
2 tablespoons of brown sugar
1/2 cup of cayenne pepper sauce
1 tablespoon of Worcestershire sauce
4 lb chicken wings

Instructions:

1. Preheat the oven to 380F.
2. Add the first 5 ingredients to a bowl and stir until well mixed.
3. Place chicken wings in the baking sheet and bake for 25 minutes, toss halfway through.
4. Increase heat to 400F and cook for an additional 5 minutes.
5. Remove from heat and serve with prepared sauce.

53

GREECE CHICKEN BBQ SKEWERS

Prep Time: 2 hours minutes
Cook Time: 20 minutes
Calories per Serving: 232
Serves: 4

Ingredients:

1/2 teaspoon of salt
1/2 teaspoon of lemon zest
2 teaspoons of dried oregano
1/4 teaspoon of ground black pepper
1/4 teaspoon of crushed dried rosemary
1 (8 oz) can of fat free plain yoghurt
2 tablespoons of freshly squeezed lemon juice
1/3 cup of crumbled feta cheese with basil and tomatoes
1 lb. Chicken breasts, boneless & skinless
1 medium red onion, chopped into wedges
1 green bell pepper, chopped to 1/2 inch pieces
*Requires wooden skewers

Instructions:

1. First chop the chicken into 1 inch pieces.
2. Add the first 8 ingredients in a bowl and stir to combine.

Add the chicken and place in the fridge to marinate for at least 2 hours.

3. Meanwhile, place skewers in water for 30 minutes.

4. Preheat the oven to 360F, thread the chicken, onions and bell pepper in the wooden skewers.

5. Work in batches if necessary, place chicken in the skewer rack and cook for 10-12 minutes, turn skewers halfway through.

54

TASTY JERK CHICKEN WINGS

Prep Time: 10 minutes
Cook Time: 30 minutes
Total Time: 40 minutes
Calories per Serving: 374
Serves: 6

Ingredients:

1 teaspoon of salt
4 chopped scallions
1 teaspoon of white pepper
1/2 cup of red wine vinegar
2 tablespoons of brown sugar
1 tablespoon of chopped thyme
1 teaspoon of cayenne pepper
1 teaspoon of cinnamon
1 tablespoon of all spice
2 tablespoon of soy sauce
2 tablespoon of olive oil
1 tablespoon of ginger, grated
5 tablespoon of fresh lime juice
1 habanera pepper, seeds removed

6 cloves of garlic, chopped

4 lb. of chicken wings

Instructions:

1. Add all ingredients except the chicken into a large mixing bowl add chicken wings and chill for at least 3 hours to marinate.

2. Preheat your oven to 390F.

3. Drain excess liquid from chicken, divide the chicken wings in half and place in the baking sheet. Transfer to the oven to cook for 15 minutes, flip sides halfway through.

4. Remove from heat and repeat with the remaining wings, enjoy!

55

TURKEY RICE WITH BROCCOLI

Prep Time: 15 minutes
Cook Time: 45 minutes
Total Time: 60 minutes
Calories per Serving: 269
Serves: 4

Ingredients:

10 oz of frozen broccoli, thawed
1/2 cup of white rice, uncooked
1/2 cup of shredded cheddar cheese
7 oz of whole wheat cracker, crushed
1 cup of cooked, turkey meat, chopped
1 tablespoon and 1 1/2 teaspoon of butter, melted

Instructions:

1. Preheat the oven to 360F

2. Add 2 cups of water in a saucepan and bring to a boil. Reduce heat to low, add rice and simmer for 20 minutes.

3. Lightly grease baking sheet with cooking spray. Add rice, turkey, cheese and broccoli to a bowl and toss to combine, transfer to the baking sheet and set aside.

4. Next, combine butter and crackers in a small bowl, spread over the rice.

5. Transfer the baking sheet to the oven and cook for 20 minutes until the tops are lightly browned, remove from heat and set aside to cool and then serve, enjoy!

56

CHICKEN CRUNCHIES WITH LEMON MAYO

Prep Time: 30 minutes
Cook Time: 75 minutes
Calories per Serving: 519
Serves: 6

Ingredients:

2 1/2 cups soft wholegrain breadcrumbs
1 3/4 lb. skinless chicken breast fillets, trimmed
3/4 cup buttermilk
1/3 cup parmesan cheese, grated
2 teaspoons of dried Italian herbs
Cracked black pepper, to season
Canola oil spray
1/2 cup of mayonnaise
1 small clove garlic, crushed
1 tablespoon lemon juice
1 tablespoon fresh parsley, chopped
Steamed jacket potatoes, to serve
Garden salad, to serve

Instructions:

1. To make the bread crumbs, process torn day-old wholegrain bread in a food processor.

2. Cut the chicken into strips, add together with buttermilk, cover and chill in a bowl for an hour.

3. Preheat oven to 400°F

4. On tray, add together the breadcrumbs, Italian herbs and parmesan. Season with pepper.

5. Remove chilled chicken from buttermilk, dredge in breadcrumb mixture to coat, and then paper-lined oven trays. Chill 15 minutes.

6. Remove from refrigerator, spritz with cooking spray and bake 20 minutes, turning halfway through.

7. Add together mayonnaise, lemon juice, the garlic and parsley.

8. Serve the cooked chicken with the lemon mayo mix, steamed potatoes and salad.

SEAFOOD

57

OVEN-ROASTED SEA BASS WITH GINGER AND LIME SAUCE

Prep Time: 10 minutes
Cook Time: 15 minutes
Total Time: 25 minutes
Serves: 2

Ingredients:

5 teaspoons of olive oil
1 tablespoon of minced shallot
1 1/2 tablespoons of soy sauce
2 tablespoons of fresh lime juice
1 tablespoon of fresh cilantro, chopped
1 tablespoon of fresh ginger, peeled & chopped
2 (6 oz.) of sea bass fillets, 3/4 inch thick
Salt and pepper to taste

Instructions:

1. Preheat oven to 400F, evenly brush a pie dish with about 2 teaspoons of olive oil and set aside.

2. Combine the lime juice, soy sauce, cilantro, ginger, minced shallot and 3 teaspoons of olive oil in a bowl. Season with salt and pepper.

3. Place fish in the prepared dish, season with salt and pepper and coat with 1/2 tablespoon of the prepared sauce.

4. Transfer to the preheated oven and roast for about 12-15 minutes until just opaque in the center. Top with the remaining sauce and serve.

58

BAKED SARDINES WITH GARLIC AND OREGANO

Prep Time: 10 minutes
Cook Time: 40 minutes
Total Time: 50 minutes
Calories per Serving: 341
Serves: 6

Ingredients:

1/2 cup of water
1/2 cup of fresh lemon juice
5 cloves of garlic, sliced thinly
1/2 cup of extra virgin olive oil
2 tablespoons of Greek oregano (rigani)
Salt and freshly ground black pepper to taste
2 1/2 lbs. of fresh sardines, scales and intestines removed

Instructions:

1. Preheat oven to 325F

2. Add all ingredients except the sardines in a bowl and stir to mix well.

3. Place sardines in a baking pan and top with the sauce mixture, coat thoroughly and evenly.

4. Transfer to the oven and bake for about 30-40 minutes until the fish is golden and the skin crisp. Enjoy!

59

SHRIMP SCAMPI BAKE

Prep Time: 30 minutes
Cook Time: 15 minutes
Calories per Serving: 420
Serves: 6

Ingredients

1 cup butter
2 tablespoons homemade Dijon-style mustard
1 tablespoon fresh lemon juice
1 tablespoon garlic, chopped
1 tablespoon fresh parsley, chopped
2 lb. medium raw shrimp, shelled, deveined, tails on

Instruction:

1. Preheat oven to 400F.

2. Melt butter in a small pan. Add the mustard, the lemon juice, the garlic and parsley. Melt once butter is completely melted.

3. Place the shrimp in a baking pan and pour butter mixture over.

4. Bake for 12 minutes.

60

LEMON PEPPER SALMON

Prep Time: 15minutes
Cook Time: 15 minutes
Total Time: 30 minutes
Calories per Serving: 190
Serves: 4

Ingredients:

1/4 teaspoon of salt
1 lb. salmon fillet, skin removed
1/4 teaspoon of cracked black pepper
1 tablespoon of butter with olive oil
1 tablespoon of lemon zest, freshly grated
1 tablespoon of lemon juice, freshly squeezed
Lemon wedges, optional
Fresh parsley sprigs, if desired

Instructions:

1. Heat oven to 375F and line a rimmed baking pan with aluminum foil.

2. Place salmon in the prepared baking pan, sprinkle with the salt,pepper,and butter with olive oil and top with lemon juice.

3. Transfer to the oven and bake for 12-15 minutes until the salmon flakes when scrapped with a fork. Remove from heat and set aside to cool for a few minutes.

4. Transfer to a plate and serve with lemon wedges and parsley if desired.

61

ROAST MOROCCAN FISH AND VEGETABLES WITH SPICY COUSCOUS

Prep Time: 15 minutes
Cook Time: 35 minutes
Total Time: 50 minutes
Serves: 6

Ingredients:
1/2 teaspoon of salt
1/2 teaspoon of pepper
10 shallots, peeled & halved vertically
2 tablespoons of extra virgin olive oil
1/4 cup of chopped Italian parsley
1 teaspoon of salt
1/4 cup of cilantro
2 teaspoons of paprika
2 cloves of garlic, minced
4 carrots, diagonally sliced
2 teaspoons of ground cumin
1 teaspoon of lemon zest, grated
2 zucchini; chopped
2 1/2 cups of chicken broth
1 teaspoon of crushed red-pepper flakes

2 lbs. of cod filets, trimmed & cubed

5 plum tomatoes, seeded and chopped

20 oz of couscous

Lemon wedges, optional

Instructions:

1. Preheat oven to 400F, lightly coat a 3-Quart casserole dish with cooking spray and set aside.

2. Combine the shallots, olive oil, salt and pepper in a bowl, toss to mix well and afterwards place in the prepared casserole dish and bake for 10 minutes.

3. While it bakes, combine the garlic, cumin, pepper, lemon zest and salt in a bowl, divide in two and season the cod fillets with half of the mixture.

4. After the casserole is baked, remove from the oven and add the carrots, tomatoes and zucchini. Stir to combine then top with the cod fillets.

5. Place casserole dish in the oven and bake until the fish is cooked and the vegetables are tender, about 20-25 minutes.

6. Meanwhile, prepare couscous following package instructions except substitute the water with broth and the earlier reserved herb mixture as seasoning.

7. Divide couscous with fish and vegetables garnished with lemon wedges if desired.

62

BAKED SOLE WITH MINT AND GINGER

Prep Time: 15 minutes
Cook Time: 25 minutes
Total Time: 40 minutes
Serves: 4

Ingredients:

1/2 teaspoon of salt
1 small bunch of mint
1 tablespoon of olive oil
2 lb. of sole fillets
1 2-inch piece ginger, peeled & chopped
1/4 teaspoon of freshly ground black pepper

Instructions:

1. Preheat oven to 375F. Lightly coat a rimmed baking pan with cooking spray and set aside.

2. Combine the rest of the ingredients in a blender and pulse until it forms a smooth paste, add a tablespoon of warm water if paste is too thick.

3. Thoroughly coat the fish fillets with paste and arrange neatly in the prepared baking pan.

4. Place in the oven and bake for about 15-20 minutes until the fish is opaque and flakes easily in the center.

5. Remove from heat and serve with rice, enjoy!

63

BAKED SWORDFISH STEAKS

Prep Time: 15 minutes
Cook Time: 25 minutes
Total Time: 40 minutes
Calories per Serving: 399
Serves: 4

Ingredients:

4 swordfish steaks
1/2 green bell pepper
2 tablespoons of olive oil
2 large bay leaves, halved
1 rib celery, finely chopped
2 tablespoons of lemon juice
4 oz. mushrooms, sliced thinly
1 cup of onions, sliced thinly
A pinch of kosher salt
A pinch of pepper
1/2 teaspoon of Creole seasoning blend
2 large ripe tomatoes, sliced thickly
3 to 4 tablespoons of vegetable broth

Instructions:

1. Preheat the oven to 350F, lightly grease a large shallow baking pan with cooking spray and set aside.
2. Slice the bell pepper in half, remove seeds and finely chop the first half of the pepper.
3. Heat the olive oil in a skillet set over medium heat, add onions, mushrooms, green bell pepper and celery to the skillet and cook for about 10 minutes until the vegetables are tender and cooked.
4. Next, add the lemon juice and season with salt and pepper, cook for 2-3 minutes. Stir regularly.
5. Spread half of the onion mixture in the prepared saucepan, top with swordfish steaks, Creole seasoning, bay leaf, tomatoes, the remaining onion mixture and vegetable broth.
6. Tent the pan tightly with foil and place in the oven to bake for about 20-25 minutes until the fish is opaque and flakes easily.

64

CRAB STUFFED HADDOCK

Prep Time: 15 minutes
Cook Time: 25 minutes
Total Time: 40 minutes
Calories per Serving: 364
Serves: 6

Ingredients:

1 egg, beaten
1/4 teaspoon salt
1/2 cup grated Romano cheese
2 tablespoons lemon juice
1 teaspoon of minced garlic
1 celery stalk, finely chopped
3 green onions, finely chopped
1/4 teaspoon ground black pepper
3 tablespoons of extra virgin olive oil
1 (6 ounce) can of lump crabmeat, drained
3 slices dry white bread, crusts removed and cubed
1 tomato, seeded and diced
1 teaspoon ground black pepper
5 tablespoons of butter, melted

6 haddock fillets, (4 ounce each)

Instructions:

1. Preheat the oven to 350 F, lightly grease a baking dish with cooking spray and set aside.

2. Heat olive oil in a skillet set over medium heat, add green onions, garlic, celery and cook for a few minutes until tender.

3. Remove from heat and stir in the bread cubes, egg, lemon juice, crab meat, Romano and tomato. Season with salt and pepper and stir until well combined.

4. Brush the haddock fillets with melted butter and arrange neatly in the prepared baking dish, top with crab mixture and loosely tent the dish with foil.

5. Place in the oven and bake for 15-20 minutes until the fish is opaque and flakes easily with a fork.

65

DIJON BAKED SALMON

Prep Time: 5 minutes

Cook Time: 20 minutes

Total Time: 25 minutes

Calories per Serving: 249

Serves: 4

Ingredients:

1 1/2 lbs salmon

1/4 cup of Dijon mustard

1 tablespoon of avocado oil

3 cloves of garlic, finely chopped

1/4 cup of fresh parsley, finely chopped

1 tablespoon of freshly squeezed lemon juice

Salt and pepper

Instructions:

1. Preheat the oven to 350 F, line a baking tray with foil and set aside.

2. Combine all ingredients except the salmon in a small bowl, stir until well mixed.

3. Place salmon in the prepared baking tray and coat with the mixture.

4. Place in the oven and bake for 15-20 minutes until it flakes easily with a fork. Remove from heat and serve.

66

BROILED TILAPIA PARMESAN

Prep Time: 10 minutes

Cook Time: 12 minutes

Total Time: 22 minutes

Calories per Serving: 177

Serves: 4

Ingredients:

1/4 cup of Parmesan cheese

2 tablespoons of butter, softened

1 tablespoon and 1 teaspoons low-fat mayonnaise

1 tablespoon of fresh lemon juice

1/8 teaspoon of dried basil

1/8 teaspoon of ground black pepper

1/8 teaspoon of onion powder

1/8 teaspoon of celery seed

1 lb tilapia fillets

Instructions:

1. Preheat your oven's broiler; line a baking pan with aluminum foil.

2. Combine all ingredients except the fillets in a bowl and stir to mix well.

3. Place fillets in the prepared baking pan and place in the oven to broil for 6 minutes, flip sides halfway through.

4. Remove from heat and pour the cheese mixture into the pan, covering the fillets, return to the oven and broil for 5 minutes until the top is browned and the fish flakes easily.

67

BAKED SCALLOPS

Prep Time: 10 minutes
Cook Time: 25 minutes
Total Time: 35 minutes
Calories per Serving: 296
Serves: 6

Ingredients:

1/2 teaspoon of sea salt
1 teaspoon of garlic powder
1 teaspoon of dried parsley
1/2 teaspoon of black pepper
1/2 cup grated Parmesan cheese
2 tablespoons of dry white wine
1 tablespoon of fresh lemon juice
6 tablespoons of unsalted butter, melted
1/8 teaspoon of cayenne pepper
2 lb. large sea scallops
1/4 teaspoon of sweet paprika
1/4 cup of Parmesan cheese, for topping

Instructions:

1. Preheat the oven to 325F, lightly grease a casserole dish with cooking spray and set aside.
2. Combine the first 9 ingredients in a bowl and stir until well mixed, sit for 5 minutes until the mixture thickens.
3. Place the scallops in the casserole dish and top with the prepared mixture.
4. Loosely tent casserole dish with foil and transfer to the oven to bake for about 20-25 minutes until cooked through and opaque, an internal temperature should read 115F.
5. Remove foil and top with the remaining parmesan and paprika and broil for 2-3 minutes until brown. Remove from heat and set aside to cool before serving, enjoy!

68

BAKED MEXICAN FISH

Prep Time: 10 minutes
Cook Time: 25 minutes
Calories per Serving: 320
Serves: 4

Ingredients:
4 (1 lb.) tilapia fillets
1 teaspoon of chili powder
2 tomatoes, thinly sliced
3 cloves of minced garlic
1/2 cup of fresh cilantro
1/4 cup of Italian Dressing
1/2 cup of shredded Mexican cheese
1/2 small red onion, thinly sliced
1 small jalapeño pepper, thinly sliced
2-2/3 cups of cooked long-grain brown rice
1 lime, quartered

Instructions:
1. Heat your oven to 400F and spray a 13x9-inch baking dish with cooking spray.

2. Arrange fish neatly in the baking dish and top with chili powder, tomatoes, onions, peppers, garlic and Italian dressing.

3. Place in the oven and bake for about 15-20 minutes until the fish is opaque and flakes easily with a fork.

4. Top with cheese and heat for 2-3 minutes until melted.

5. Remove from heat and serve with rice, lime and cilantro, enjoy!

69

BAKED TILAPIA WITH BUTTERY CRUMB TOPPING

Prep Time: 10 minutes

Cook Time: 25 minutes

Total Time: 35 minutes

Calories per Serving: 372

Serves: 4

Ingredients:

4 tilapia fillets (1 1/2 pounds)

1 cup of bread crumbs

Salt and pepper to taste

1/2 teaspoon of dried basil

3 tablespoons of melted butter

Instructions:

1. Heat your oven to 375F and lightly coat a large baking dish with butter.

2. Combine the butter with basil and breadcrumbs, set aside.

3. Next, arrange the fillets neatly in the prepared baking dish, season with salt, pepper and sprinkle bread crumbs over the fillets.

4. Place fillets in the oven to bake for 12-15 minutes until fish is cooked through and crumbs are lightly browned. Enjoy!

VEGETABLES

70

TASTY JALAPENO POPPERS

Prep Time: 10 minutes
Cook Time: 10 minutes
Total Time: 20 minutes
Calories per Serving: 240
Serves: 4

Ingredients:

14 fresh jalapenos, sliced lengthwise
1 cup of nonfat refried beans
1 cup of shredded cheddar cheese
1 scallion, chopped
1 teaspoon of salt, divided
1/4 cups of flour
2 eggs, beaten
1/2 cup of corn flour
Cooking spray

Instructions:

1. Place Jalapenos in a microwavable bowl and microwave for 5 minutes until soft. Remove from heat and scoop out the seeds, set aside.

2. Next, combine the beans, cheese, scallions and 1/2 teaspoon of salt in a mixing bowl.

3. Scoop a tablespoon of bean mixture and press into jalapenos, press jalapeno close and set aside.

4. Place the corn flour and the remaining 1/2 teaspoon of salt in a bowl, place flour in a separate bowl and set aside.

5. Arrange the egg, cornmeal and flour bowl assembly line style; Dredge pepper first in the flour, then the egg and finally the corn flour. Ensure it is well coated.

6. Place on a baking sheet and lightly coat with a few squirts of cooking spray. Transfer to the middle shelf of the oven and cook for 10 minutes with temperature set to 400F. Halfway through remove from the oven and flip sides.

71

NUTTY CAULIFLOWER BITES

Prep Time: 10 minutes
Cook Time: 20 minutes
Total Time: 30 minutes
Calories per Serving: 144
Serves: 4

Ingredients:

1/3 cup of oats flour
1/3 cup of plain flour
1/3 cup of desiccated coconut
Salt and pepper to taste
1 tablespoon of flaxseed meal
3 tablespoons of warm water
1 medium cauliflower, cut into florets
1 teaspoon of mixed spice
1/2 teaspoon of mustard powder
2 tablespoons of maple syrup
1 clove of minced garlic
2 tablespoons of soy sauce

Instructions:

1. Preheat the oven to 400F and lightly coat and baking sheet with cooking spray.
2. Combine the first 3 ingredients in a mixing bowl and season with salt and pepper, set aside.
3. Prepare the flax egg; Combine flaxseed meal, three tablespoons of warm water and a pinch of salt in a small bowl, stir to mix well.
4. In a separate bowl, combine the cauliflower florets, mixed spice and mustard powder, mix well and set aside.
5. Line the bowls assembly line style; Dredge the florets first in the flax egg mixture, then in the flour mixture. Place neatly in the baking sheet and transfer to the preheated oven to cook for 15 minutes.
6. While the cauliflower roasts, combine the maple syrup, garlic and soy sauce in a saucepan set over medium heat and bring to a boil.
7. Reduce heat to low and simmer until the sauce thickens.
8. Remove florets from the oven and place in the saucepan, stir to coat well.
9. Transfer the mixture back to the oven and heat for 3-5 minutes before serving.

72

ROAST CAULIFLOWER AND BROCCOLI FLORETS WITH GARLIC DIPPING SAUCE

Prep Time: 10 minutes
Cook Time: 30 minutes

Ingredients:
1 small cauliflower head, cut into florets
1 small brocolli head, cut into florets
Salt and freshly ground black pepper
For the Dipping Sauce:
4 tablespoons of butter, room temp.
2 tablespoons of olive oil
2 cloves of garlic, minced
1 tablespoon of anchovy paste

Instructions:
1. Preheat the oven to 225F and line two rimless baking sheets with parchment paper
2. Arrange the broccoli and cauliflower neatly in the prepared baking sheet, sprinkle salt and pepper over them.
3. Place the pans in the oven and bake for 30 minutes until crisp and tender.
4. While the vegetables roast, prepare the dipping sauce; combine all ingredients to a bowl and stir until well mixed.

5. Place in a saucepan and heat for 30 seconds or more until slightly warm, remove and set aside.

6. Transfer roasted vegetables to a serving bowl and serve with dipping sauce, enjoy!

73

TASTY JICAMA FRIES

Prep Time: 10 minutes
Cook Time: 5 minutes
Total Time: 15 minutes
Calories per Serving: 210
Serves: 8

Ingredients:

4 eggs, beaten
1/2 of a large jicama
1 tablespoon of dried thyme
3/4 cups of arrowroot flour

Instructions:

1. Lightly coat a baking sheet with olive oil, set aside.

2. Slice jicama into 1/4 inch fry-like strips.

3. Place eggs in a large bowl and top with jicama strips, toss to coat well, set aside.

4. Combine the rest of the ingredients in a bowl and stir to mix well. Add coated jicama to the dry bowl mixture and toss until well coated.

5. Place coated jicama on prepared baking sheet and transfer

to the oven, set temperature to 350F and cook for 5 minutes until set. Enjoy!

74

ASPARAGUS STRATA

Prep Time: 10 minutes
Cook Time: 15 minutes
Total Time: 25 minutes
Calories per Serving: 166
Serves: 4

Ingredients:

4 medium eggs, beaten
3 tablespoons of whole milk
1/2 cup of Swiss cheese, grated
6 asparagus spears, chopped into 2 inch bits
Salt and freshly ground black pepper to taste
2 slices of whole wheat bread, sliced to 1/2 inch cubes

Instructions:

1. Add a tablespoon of warm water to a 6 inch baking pan and top with the asparagus spears.

2. Transfer the asparagus to the oven with temperature set to 350F and bake for 5 minutes until soft and tender. Remove and set aside. Drain fluids from the pan if any.

3. Lightly coat the pan with cooking spray, add asparagus and bread crumbs to the pan and set aside.

4. Next, combine eggs, milk and the rest of the ingredients to a mixing bowl and stir to mix well.

5. Add mixture to the baking pan and place in the oven. Set temperature to 360F and cook for 10-15 minutes until the eggs are soft and browned. Check doneness by inserting a toothpick to the center until it comes out clean.

75

BAKED BRUSSELS SPROUTS

Oven Baked Asparagus
 Prep Time: 5 minutes
 Cook Time: 10 minutes
 Total Time: 13 minutes
 Calories per Serving: 17
 Serves: 2

Ingredients:
Olive oil
A medium sized bunch of asparagus

Instructions:

1. Wash the asparagus and dry with paper towels, trim off the ends

2. Lightly and evenly coat with olive oil and sprinkle with yeast.

3. Arrange neatly in the baking dish and place in the oven to heat with temperature set to 360F and time to 8 minutes.

76

ALMOND FLOUR ONION RINGS

Prep Time: 5 minutes
Cook Time: 15 minutes
Total Time: 20 minutes
Calories per Serving: 217
Serves: 3

Ingredients:

1 egg, beaten
3/4 cup of coconut milk
1/2 cup of almond flour
Salt and pepper to taste
1 tablespoon of smoked paprika
1 tablespoon of baking powder
1 medium sized onion, sliced into rings

Instructions:

1. Combine the almond flour, paprika, baking powder and salt and pepper to a mixing bowl and stir until well combined, set aside.

2. In another bowl, combine the eggs, onions and coconut and stir until onions are well soaked.

3. Remove onion slices from the egg mixture and dredge in almond flour until well coated.

4. Pour the mixture to the baking dish and place in the oven with temperature set to 325F. Cook for 10-15 minutes until evenly browned.

77

AVOCADO FRIES

Prep Time: 10 minutes
Cook Time: 7 minutes
Total Time: 17 minutes
Calories per Serving: 100
Serves: 6

Ingredients:

1/2 teaspoon of salt
1/2 cup of panko breadcrumbs
1 medium avocado, peeled, pitted & sliced
Drained bean liquid from a 15 oz. can of white beans

Instructions:

1. Combine the salt and panko breadcrumbs in a mixing bowl, set aside.

2. Place the bean liquid in another bowl.

3. Dredge avocado slices first in the bean liquid, then coat with the panko mixture.

4. Arrange neatly in a baking sheet and transfer to the oven with temperature set to 380F. Cook for 5 minutes.

5. Remove from the oven and serve with preferred dipping sauce.

78

ROASTED VEGETABLE SALAD

Prep Time: 20 minutes
Cook Time: 60 minutes
Serves: 3

Ingredients:

3 medium zucchini
Fresh basil leaves
2 teaspoon of salt
1 tablespoon of olive oil
4 cups of one shaped pasta
1/2 cup of Italian dressing
6 tablespoons of grated parmesan
1 cup of tomatoes, finely chopped
2 tablespoons of olive oil, divided
4 medium tomatoes, sliced into eights
2 medium green pepper, finely chopped
3 medium eggplant, rinsed & sliced to 1/2 inch rounds

Instructions:

1. Place the eggplants in a bowl, add a tablespoon of olive oil and toss until well coated.

2. Transfer to a baking sheet and place in the oven with

temperature set to 360F, cook for 40 minutes until it soft and creamy.

3. While eggplant cooks, rinse the zucchini and slice off the green ends. Slice the remaining parts into 1/2 inch thick rounds and place in a bowl and coat with the remaining tablespoon of olive oil, set aside.

4. After the eggplants are cooked, add zucchini to the oven and cook for 25 minutes until it turns golden brown, set aside.

5. Arrange sliced tomatoes, cut side up in the baking dish, place in the oven and cook for 20 minutes.

6. While the tomatoes roasts, prepare the pasta following the package instructions afterwards, drain in a colander and rinse with cold water, set aside.

7. Add the pepper, tomatoes, pasta, roasted vegetables and the rest of the ingredients in a large mixing bowl, toss to combine and place in the refrigerator to chill for a few minutes before serving.

79

ROASTED BRUSSELS SPROUTS

Prep Time: 10 minutes
Cook Time: 10 minutes
Total Time: 20 minutes
Calories per Serving: 118
Serves: 8

Ingredients:
1/4 teaspoon of salt
2 cups of Brussels sprouts
1 tablespoon of balsamic vinegar
1 tablespoon of extra virgin olive oil

Instructions:
1. Slice Brussels in half lengthwise and transfer to a bowl.
2. Add the rest of the ingredients to the bowl and toss until well combined.
3. Place in a baking pan and transfer to the oven, set temperature to 400F and roast for 10 minutes until brown and crisp, halfway through cooking remove from heat and toss.

80

ROASTED BROCCOLI

Prep Time: 10 minutes
Cook Time: 8 minutes
Total Time: 18 minutes
Calories Per Serving: 96
Serves: 2

Ingredients:

1/2 teaspoon of salt
1/4 teaspoon of masala spice
2 tablespoon of yogurt
1/4 teaspoon of turmeric
1/2 teaspoon of chili powder
1 tablespoon of chickpea flour
1 lb. broccoli, cut into florets

Instructions:

1. Combine all ingredients except florets in a large mixing bowl and stir until well mixed.

2. Add florets to the marinade mixture, transfer to the fridge and chill for 30-45 minutes.

3. Preheat the oven to 350F.

4. Remove florets from the fridge and place marinated florets in the fryer basket and roast for 10 minutes until crispy.

81

PINEAPPLE COCONUT BROWN RICE SALAD

Prep Time: 10 minutes
Cook Time: 5 minutes
Calories per Serving: 468
Serves: 6

Ingredients

½ pineapple
Baby spinach
1 red capsicum
Handful fresh mint
Cracked black pepper
Juice of half a lemon
½ cup of shredded coconut
Handful fresh flat leaf parsley
2 tablespoons extra virgin olive oil
2 pkt. brown rice

Instructions:

1. Preheat your oven to 300°F. Place the coconut on a sheet pan and roast 3-5 minutes, stirring 2-3 times until light brown. Remove from heat and set aside.

2. Cook the brown rice as directed on the package.

3. Next, prepare your fruits and vegetables: remove peel from pineapple, core and cut into small pieces. Dice the red capsicum, discarding the seeds and core. Chop the fresh herbs roughly.

4. Combine all in a salad bowl, toss well to mix and serve.

DESSERT AND APPETIZERS

82

ROASTED BBQ CHICKPEAS

Prep Time: 5 minutes
Cook Time: 22 minutes
Total Time: 27 minutes
Calories Per Serving: 204
Serves: 4

Ingredients:

2 tablespoons of BBQ sauce
1/2 tablespoon melted coconut oil
15 oz. can chickpeas, drained and rinsed

Instructions

1. Preheat oven to 400F convection roast.
2. Peel off skins off chickpeas, place in a baking sheet and roast for 10 minutes, shake regularly to prevent chickpeas from sticking to one another.
3. Remove from heat, add coconut oil over the chickpeas and stir until evenly coated.
4. Next, pour the BBQ sauce over the chickpeas and toss until evenly coated.
5. Return to the baking sheet and roast for another 12 minutes, tossing halfway through.

6. Remove from heat and set aside to cool for a few minutes before serving.

83

FLAKY BUTTERMILK BISCUITS

Prep Time: 30 minutes
  Cook Time: 16 minutes
  Total Time: 46 minutes
  Total Calories: 400
  Serves: 2

Ingredients:
3/4 cup of buttermilk
3/4 teaspoon of kosher salt
1/4 teaspoon of baking soda
4 oz. of cold unsalted butter
1/4 cups of all-purpose flour
1 tablespoon of granulated sugar
2-1/4 teaspoon of baking powder

Instructions:
1. Place a rack in the middle of the oven and preheat the oven to 500°F. Line a rimmed baking sheet with foil and set aside.
2. Add the flour, sugar, baking soda =, baking powder and salt in a large mixing bowl, stir to combine.
3. Cut the butter into 6 pieces of 1/4 inch bits, evenly

distribute to the flour mixture, and ensure no two butter bit sticks together.

4. Add butter milk and stir for about a minute until it forms a coarse dough lump.

5. Sprinkle a clean, flat surface with flour and place dough on the floured surface. Dust your hands with flour and knead the dough into a 3/4-inch-thick rectangle.

6. Sprinkle a bit of flour over the dough and fold the dough into 3 parts similar to you folding a letter. Stretch out the dough again to a 3/4-inch-thick rectangle and dust again with flour, repeat the triple folding procedure two more times.

7. Next, shape the dough into a 1/2 inch thick oval and cut with a 2 inch biscuit cutter, transfer the biscuits to the prepared baking sheet, spacing them 1/2 inch apart for even cooking.

8. Place the baking sheet in the oven and reduce the temperature to 425F, bake for 8 minutes and rotate the direction of the pan, continue baking for another 6-8 minutes until the biscuit has doubled in height and evenly golden browned. Remove from heat and set aside to cool before serving.

84

BROWN SUGAR SHORTBREAD CARAMEL BARS

Prep Time: 15 minutes
Cook Time: 30 minutes
Calories per Serving: 186
Serves: 24 bars

Ingredients:

For the Caramel Filling:

3 tablespoons of butter

3 tablespoons of corn syrup

1 14 oz. can of sweetened condensed milk

For the shortbread:

3/4 cup of butter

1/2 cup of brown sugar

1 teaspoon of baking powder

1 1/2 cups of all purpose flour

Instructions:

1. Prepare the caramel filling: Add the milk, butter and corn syrup to a saucepan set over medium heat and bring to a boil. Stir constantly with a wooden spoon to prevent burning. Remove from heat and set aside to cool to room temperature.

2. Preheat the oven to 325F and line a 9x9 inch baking sheet with foil, set aside.

3. Combine the baking powder, flour, sugar and butter in a food processor and pulse until crumbly.

4. Press half of the mixture to the bottom of the pan, spread the cooled filling over the bottom layer of the pan then shape the remaining crumble in handfuls and break off into 1/2 inch pieces the size of you pinkie, scatter over the caramel layer.

5. Place baking pan in the oven and bake for 25-30 minutes until the top is golden brown, remove from heat and cool before cutting into squares.

85

SWEET SPICED PECANS

Prep Time: 5 minutes
  Cook Time: 15 minutes
  Total Time: 20 minutes
  Calories per Serving: 336 (16 servings)
  Serves: 6 cups

Ingredients:

6 cups of pecan halves
1 ½ teaspoons of cinnamon
½ teaspoon of ground ginger
¾ teaspoons of black pepper
1 ½ teaspoons of kosher salt
¾ teaspoon of cayenne pepper
5 tablespoons of butter, melted
2 tablespoons of light brown sugar

Instructions:

1. Heat oven to 325F, coat a large rimmed baking sheet with cooking spray and set aside.

2. Combine all ingredients except the butter and nuts in a small bowl. Add pecans and 2 tablespoon of butter in a small

bowl, toss to coat then transfer to the baking sheet and spread in a single layer.

3. Place in the oven and bake for about 10 minutes, transfer to a large bowl and coat with the remaining butter then return to the oven to toast for 4-5 minutes.

86

VERY BERRY PIE

Prep Time: 60 minutes
Cook Time: 60 minutes
Total Time: 120 minutes
Calories per Serving: 510
Serves: 8

Ingredients:

For the pie crust:
1/2 cup of cold water
1/4 teaspoon of nutmeg
1/4 teaspoon of cinnamon
1 1/3 cups of cold butter
4 1/4 cups flour, divided
1 1/2 teaspoons of salt

For the pie filling:
1 egg, white
1 tablespoon lemon juice
1 (16 oz) bag of frozen cranberries
2 (16 oz) bags of frozen mixed berries
1 1/2 cup sugar, plus more for sprinkling on top of the pie

Instructions:

1. Add 4 cups of flour, cinnamon, nutmeg and salt to a large mixing bowl, whisk to combine. Cut up the butter into small pieces and whisk until the butter is broken up in the dough.

2. Stir in the ice water with a fork, stirring until the ingredients turn to dough.

3. Place the dough on a clean flat surface and shape into two equal disks, cover in a bowl and place in the fridge to chill for at least an hour.

4. After an hour, remove one of the dough disks from the fridge and place on a lightly floured clean surface. Roll the dough and transfer into a 9 inch pie plate.

5. Prepare the filling: combine the berries, sugar and lemon juice in a large pot set over medium heat and bring to a boil. Reduce heat to low and simmer for 10 minutes, stirring regularly until slightly thickened.

6. Transfer the berries to the pie pan with a slotted spoon to transfer as little moisture as possible, set aside.

7. Bring out the remaining dough disk from the fridge and place on a lightly floured surface. Roll to about 1/4 inch thickness and cut the dough into 1/2 inch wide strips with a blunt knife or a pizza wheel.

8. Lay out half of the strips over the filling across the pie with about 1/2 inch space between them, fold back every other strip and weave a long strip perpendicular to the original strip. Repeat with the next strip but with every other strip folded back until the weave is completed over the top of the pie.

9. Use a scissors to trim off any loose strips hanging over the edge, brush the top of the pie with egg whites and top with a sprinkle of granulated sugar. Wrap foil around the edge of the pie crust to prevent it from burning, set aside.

10. Preheat the oven to 375F

11. Place the pie in the oven and bake for 20 minutes then remove the foil.

12. Place in the oven and bake for another 15 minutes until the top begins to brown. Remove from heat and set aside until completely cooled before serving.

87

CHEDDAR CHEESE PUFFS

Prep Time: 10 minutes
Cook Time: 40 minutes
Serves: 2 dozen

Ingredients:
1 cup of warm water
1/2 teaspoon of salt
4 large eggs, beaten
8 tablespoons of butter
1 cup of all purpose flour
1 cup of cheddar cheese, grated
2 teaspoons of fresh thyme, finely chopped
Freshly ground pepper

Instructions:
1. Add the butter, water and salt in a small saucepan set over medium heat and bring to a boil.
2. Reduce heat to low and add the flour, stir to form a dough ball that pulls away from the side of the pan.
3. Remove from heat and cool for about 5 minutes then add eggs, stir until the egg becomes well incorporated and the dough turns creamy.

4. Next stir in the grated cheese, thyme and pepper.
5. Preheat the oven to 400F; line a baking sheet with foil.
6. Shape dough into teaspoon shaped balls and place in the baking sheet, arrange neatly with about an inch separating each ball.
7. Transfer to the oven and bake for about 10 minutes, reduce heat to 350F and continue baking until slightly puffed and golden brown for another 15 minutes

88

FETA AND ZUCCHINI FRITTERS WITH GARLIC YOGURT SAUCE

Prep Time: 15 minutes
Cook Time: 20 minutes
Total Time: 35 minutes
Calories per Serving:
Serves: 8

Ingredients:

2 eggs, beaten
1/2 cup of flour
1 teaspoon of salt
3 medium zucchini, grated
6 oz of crumbled feta cheese
1 large onion, finely chopped
1 tablespoon of butter, room temp
1/4 cup of fresh dill, finely chopped
Pepper
Olive oil
For the garlic yogurt sauce:
2 cloves of garlic
1 cup of Greek yogurt
1 tablespoon of fresh Dill

Instructions

1. Place zucchini in a colander, add a teaspoon of salt and sit for 30 minutes to drain the water out of the zucchini. Place in a paper towel and squeeze to remove the excess water. Place in a large bowl and set aside.

2. Sauté the onions in butter over low heat for 5 minutes, add onions to the zucchini bowl with cheese and dill, stir to mix well.

3. Next, combine the flour and egg in a bowl, add the zucchini mixture and combine all ingredients. Sprinkle ground pepper and stir.

4. Heat olive oil in a large skillet. Drop the zucchini mixture to the oil and fry until golden on both sides.

5. To prepare the garlic sauce: combine all ingredients in a bowl, serve with zucchini, enjoy!

BLACK & WHITE BROWNIES

Prep Time: 15 minutes
Cook Time: 20 minutes
Calories per Serving: 221
Serves: 16 brownies

Ingredients:

1/2 teaspoon of salt
2 large eggs, beaten
1/4 teaspoon of nutmeg
1 cup of chopped chocolate
3/4 cup of granulated sugar
4 tablespoons of cold butter
1/2 teaspoon of baking powder
2 teaspoons of vanilla extract
1 cup of chopped white chocolate
1 1/4 cups of all purpose flour

Instructions:

1. Preheat the oven to 325F. Lightly grease a 9 inch baking pan and set aside.

2. Add the white chocolate and butter in a microwavable

bowl, place in the microwave and heat at low power at 1 minute intervals until the chocolate softens.

3. Stir in the nutmeg, vanilla, sugar and salt in the mixture and set aside to cool.

4. Combine the flour, baking powder in a large bowl and stir in the egg mixture. Add the nutmeg mixture then 3/4 cup of chocolate chopped mixture in the flour and stir until well incorporated.

5. Spoon the batter into the baking sheet, top with the remaining chocolate chunks and place in the oven to bake for 20 minutes until light golden brown.

90

BLUEBERRY MUFFINS RECIPE WITH LEMON GLAZE

Prep Time: 10 minutes
Cook Time: 30 minutes
Total Time: 40 minutes
Serves: 8 muffins

Ingredients:

1 large egg
5 oz. of sugar
2 ½ oz of milk
¼ teaspoon of salt
½ cup of canola oil
¼ cup of plain yogurt
1 tablespoon of lemon zest
1 teaspoon of baking powder
1 teaspoon of vanilla extract
1 ¼ cups of all-purpose flour
1 cup of fresh blueberries

Instructions:

1. Preheat the oven to 350F, line 8 muffin cups with paper liners and set aside.

2. Combine the egg, oil, milk, sugar, lemon zest, yogurt and vanilla in a bowl.

3. In a separate bowl, combine the baking powder, flour and salt in a bowl. Mix both bowls until well combined. Add blueberries to the mixture.

4. Transfer the batter into the muffin cups until almost full.

5. Place in the middle rack of the oven and bake for 30-35 minutes until a toothpick inserted in the center of a muffin cup comes out clean.

6. Remove from heat and set aside to cool for a few minutes before serving.

91

APPLE HAND PIES

Prep Time: 2 hours
Cook Time: 35 minutes
Total Time: 2 hours 35 minutes
Calories per Serving: 175
Serves: 15 hand pies

Ingredients:
½ teaspoon of salt
½ cup of sour cream
½ cup of cold water
2½ cups of all-purpose flour
4 teaspoons of fresh lemon juice
1 cup of unsalted butter, chilled & cut into small pieces
1 egg yolk
Coarse Sugar
2 tablespoons of warm water
For the filling:
½ teaspoon of ground cinnamon
2 large apples, peeled, cored & diced
Cup of granulated sugar
A Pinch of salt

Instructions:

1. Combine the flour and salt in a large bowl, add the bowl and whisk until it resembles a coarse meal.

2. Combine the sour cream, lemon juice and water in a bowl. Add to the flour mixture and stir until large lumps form and flour has been moistened.

3. Pat the dough with your hands into a ball and wrap in plastic wrap. Place in the fridge to chill for at least an hour.

4. To prepare the pies, line a baking sheet with foil and set aside.

5. Divide the dough in half and place on a clean lightly floured surface, roll out the dough until inch thick and cut into circles with a 4 inch biscuit cutter. Repeat with the remaining half of the dough then transfer cut dough to the prepared baking pan.

6. Place the baking pan in the fridge to chill for 30 minutes.

7. Meanwhile, to prepare the filling combine the apples, cinnamon, salt and sugar in a saucepan set over low heat and cook for 7-10 minutes until the apples are tender

8. Remove the dough from the fridge and spoon about 1-1 1/2 tablespoon of filling to each dough circle.

9. Sprinkle a few drops of water of the dough then fold in half, creating a semi circle. Seal the pie by pressing the ends of the dough with the tines of a fork.

10. Place in the fridge to chill for about 30 minutes.

11. Preheat the oven to 350F.

12. Combine the egg yolk and water in a small bowl. Brush the hand pies with the egg yolk using a cooking brush. Cut small slits on the top of the pies then sprinkle sugar into the slits.

13. Place in the oven and bake for 25-35 minutes until golden brown. Remove from the oven and set aside to cool before serving..

92

EASY BAKED GLAZED CHOCOLATE DONUTS

Prep Time: 10 minutes
Cook Time: 10 minutes
Total Time: 20 minutes
Calories per Serving: 256
Serves: 8 doughnuts

Ingredients:

1 large egg, beaten
1/8 teaspoon of salt
1/2 cup of buttermilk
1 teaspoon of vanilla
1 cup of all-purpose flour
1/2 cup of granulated sugar
1/2 teaspoon of baking soda
2 tablespoons of melted butter
1/4 cup of unsweetened cocoa powder
For the chocolate glaze:
4 tablespoons of milk
1 cup of powdered sugar
1/2 teaspoon of vanilla
3 tablespoons of unsweetened cocoa powder

Instructions:

1. Preheat the oven to 325F, line the doughnut pan with non stick cooking spray and set aside.

2. Combine the flour, baking soda, cocoa powder and salt in a large mixing bowl.

3. Combine the buttermilk, butter, vanilla, egg and sugar in a separate. Transfer the mixture to the bowl containing the baking soda and stir to mix well.

4. Spoon the batter into the doughnut cavities, ensuring it is not all the way full.

5. Place in the oven and bake for 8-10 minutes until a toothpick inserted in the center comes out clean.

6. Meanwhile, prepare the glaze: Combine all ingredients into a bowl. If the glaze is too thick, add a tablespoon of milk at a time until it reaches your preferred consistency.

7. Brush the glaze over the doughnuts while it is still hot and transfer to a wire rack to cool.

93

RASPBERRY CREAM CHEESE SWEET ROLLS

Prep Time: 2 hours
Cook Time: 15 minutes
Total Time: 2 hours 15 minutes
Calories per Serving: 419
Serves: 8 rolls

Ingredients:

1 egg, beaten
2 cups of flour
1/2 cup warm milk
3 tablespoons sugar
1/2 teaspoon of salt
1/2 tablespoon of instant yeast
1/4 cup butter, room temperature
For the Cream Cheese Filling
4 ounces cream cheese, softened
2 tablespoons butter, softened
1/4 cup granulated sugar
1 teaspoon vanilla
For the Raspberry Filling
1 1/2 cups of frozen raspberries

1/2 tablespoon cornstarch
Cream Cheese Glaze
1 oz of cream cheese
1/2 teaspoon vanilla
2-4 tablespoons of milk
3/4 cup of powdered sugar
1/4 cup of butter, softened

Instructions:

1. Proof the yeast in the warm milk for 5-10 minutes until it forms a creamy foam. Add the sugar, salt, butter and egg and flour and whisk until it forms a thick dough.

2. Place the dough on a smooth floured surface and knead until smooth and stretchy. Place in a greased medium sized bowl and set aside until it rises almost double in size.

3. Meanwhile, prepare the cream cheese filling: Combine the butter, cream cheese and sugar until smooth, add the vanilla and stir. Combine the raspberry and cornstarch in a bowl.

4. Roll the dough on a smooth surface into a rectangle about 10 by 18 inch in size. Spread the cream cheese mixture and top with the raspberry mixture. Grab by the short edge and roll tightly to the other end.

5. Cut the logs into 7-9 rolls and transfer to a baking pan, sit for a few minutes until they rise, almost double in size.

6. Preheat the oven to 350F and bake for 15 minutes until crisp and not doughy. Let the rolls cool a little before drizzling with glaze.

94

GINGER SPICE COOKIES

Prep Time: 15 minutes
Cook Time: 12 minutes
Total Time: 27 minutes
Calories per Serving: 97
Serves: 30 cookies

Ingredients:
1 large egg, beaten
3/4 teaspoon of salt
1 cup of dark brown sugar
2 teaspoon of baking soda
1 teaspoon of ground cloves
2 cups of all purpose flour
1 teaspoon of ground cinnamon
2 1/2 teaspoon of ground ginger
1/4 cup of unsalted butter, room temp
3/4 cup of chopped crystallized ginger
1/2 cup of vegetable shortening, room temp
1/4 cup of light molasses
Sugar

Instructions:

1. Combine the flour, ginger, soda, cinnamon, cloves and salt in a medium bowl, whisk to combine then add crystallized ginger.

2. Next combine the shortening, butter and brown sugar in a bowl and mix with an electric mixer until fluffy.

3. Add the eggs, molasses and whisk until well combined. Transfer the flour mixture and whisk. Cover and place in the fridge to refrigerate for at least an hour.

4. Preheat the oven to 325F, lightly coat 2 baking sheets with cooking spray/butter.

5. Spoon the sugar in a plate. Lightly wet your hands and knead the dough into 1 1/4 inch balls, roll in the sugar plate then place in the prepared baking sheet.

6. Place cookies in the oven and bake for about 12 minutes until lightly cracked on top but still soft. Place on a cooling rack to cool for a few minutes before serving.

95

VEGAN COCONUT CAKE

Prep Time: 3 hours
Cook Time: 40 minutes
Total Time: 3 hours 40 minutes
Calories per Serving: 409
Serves: 12

Ingredients:
Dry Ingredients:

1/2 teaspoon of salt
2 cups of instant oats
1 cup of coconut sugar
3/4 cup of white rice flour
1 teaspoon of baking soda
2 teaspoon of baking powder
1 1/2 cups of shredded unsweetened coconut

Wet Ingredients:

2/3 cup of apple sauce
4 tablespoons of maple syrup
1 1/3 cup of coconut milk canned
1 tablespoon of apple cider vinegar
For the Frosting:

1/3 cup of maple syrup

1/2 cup of coconut milk

2/3 cup of coconut butter

4 tablespoons of coconut rum

1 medium sized Japanese sweet potato, chopped into 1-inch cubes

Instructions:

1. Place the potato in a saucepan set over medium heat and boil until fork tender.

2. Combine the oats, shredded coconut and the rest of the dry ingredients into a blender and blend until smooth. Transfer to a large mixing bowl and set aside.

3. Next, preheat the oven to 325F. Grease and line two 8-inch cake pans with parchment paper, set aside.

4. Combine the dry ingredients into a blender and blend until smooth, transfer the mixture to the dry ingredients bowl and whisk batter until both are well combined.

5. Gently divide the batter between the two cake pans and place in the oven. Bake for 30-35 minutes until a toothpick inserted in the center comes out clean.

6. While the cake bakes, prepare the frosting; Transfer all ingredients to the blender and blend until smooth and creamy.

7. When cake has slightly cooled, frost as desired. Place in the fridge to chill for 2- 3 hours before serving..

96

CRÈME BRÛLÉE

Prep Time: 15 minutes
Cook Time: 30 minutes
Total Time: 45 minutes
Calories per Serving: 620
Serves: 4

Ingredients:
2 cups of double cream
1/2 cup of full-fat milk
5 large egg, yolks
1 vanilla pod, seed removed
4 tablespoons of raw sugar, plus extra for the topping
175ml ramekins

Instructions:
1. Heat the oven to 325F
2. Place the ramekin into a deep roasting tin; pour warm water into the tin just enough to cover the bottom of the ramekin. Ensure none gets into the ramekins and set aside.
3. Combine the eggs and sugar into a mixing bowl and whisk until fluffy, set aside.
4. Next, combine milk and vanilla pod in a medium saucepan

set over medium heat and boil. Immediately bubbles appear, remove from heat and pour to the mixing bowl with the eggs, keep stirring with the wire whisk.

5. Set a sieve and pour the mixture through to strain any loose vanilla seeds.

6. Transfer the cream to the ramekins and fill them to the top, lightly tent with foil and transfer to the oven. Bake for 25-30 minutes until softly set and not too firm.

7. Remove from the oven and set on a wire rack to cool for a few minutes.

8. Serve with a sprinkle of caster sugar over each ramekin, lightly spray with a water bottle to dampen the sugar and caramelize with a blow torch.

9. To caramelize; Hold the flame a few inches away from the ramekin and rotate the ramekin with your other hand until caramelized. Keep in the fridge to firm for at least 1 hour before serving.

97

UPSIDE-DOWN PEACH CAKE

Prep Time: 15 minutes
　　Cook Time: 35 minutes
　　Total Time: 50 minutes
　　Calories per Serving: 386 (1 slice)
　　Serves: 1 peach cake

Ingredients:

3/4 cup sugar
1/4 teaspoon salt
1/2 cup of 2% milk
1 large egg, beaten
3/4 cup of butter, divided
1 teaspoon vanilla extract
1/2 cup packed brown sugar
1 1/4 cups all-purpose flour
1 1/4 teaspoons baking powder
2 cups of fresh peaches, sliced & peeled

Instructions:

1. Preheat the oven to 325F
2. Melt 1/4 cup of butter in a saucepan, then transfer to a 9 inch baking pan and grease.

3. Sprinkle with brown sugar evenly around the baking pan, arrange peach slices in a single layer in the pan then set aside.

4. Next, combine the cream sugar and butter in a bowl, whisk until fluffy. Add the eggs and vanilla then the baking powder, flour and salt. Add milk and whisk until well combined.

5. Transfer mixture to the baking pan. Place in the oven to bake for 30-40 minutes. To check doneness, insert a toothpick in the center to check if it comes out clean.

6. Remove from heat and set aside to cool for a few minutes before serving.

www.ingramcontent.com/pod-product-compliance
Lightning Source LLC
Chambersburg PA
CBHW070106120526
44588CB00032B/1116